Bob

A Canadian in God's Own Country

Rambling, Umpiring and Golfing in North Yorkshire

R

A CANADIAN IN GOD'S OWN COUNTRY

RAMBLING, UMPIRING AND GOLFING IN NORTH YORKSHIRE

ROBIN BENGER

www.robinbenger.com

Thanks to:
Julia North
John Blackwood
Ann Thomas
Layne Coleman
Brian MacLeod Rogers
Gillie Hatton and Graeme Wilkinson

Back cover photo:
Tess Benger

Published in paperback in 2017 by Sixth Element Publishing
on behalf of Robin Benger

ISBN 978-1-912218-13-4

British Library Cataloguing in Publication Data. A catalogue record for this book is available from the British Library.

Imagine the accents. Most names are real, a few are not.

Illustrations by Graeme Wilkinson

Printed in Great Britain.

I left England when I was five and now at the age of sixty six find myself returning, asking questions about my own Britishness. My wife Nicky buys a caravan in North Yorkshire at Castle Howard. I shed my documentary company in Canada and move in for the summer of '17.

Through my walks, my golf and my cricket, I discover people, places and whoever I am beneath decades of foreign living. I walk and I walk, letting my imagination roam free, letting things come to me. It's an emptying out process, and a refilling process. As I quickly realise, North Yorkshire is a rich, friendly and beautiful place to be doing this.

What follows is a series of sketches, thoughts, encounters and joys.

Robin Benger

SATURDAY 6TH MAY

THE GREATEST LIVING YORKSHIREMAN

Well, I have been here about thirteen days, and it seems like two months.

I like it very much. Independence and freedom are big reasons.

I have my red Vauxhall which cost about six thousand pounds.

I like the music they play on BBC Radio York and the slightly banal content of its programming. Lots of Four Tops, Supremes and '60s songs.

The pro, Tony, greets me warmly when I first pop into the shop at the South Scarborough Cliff Golf Club on a sunny February day. I explain I am moving to North Yorkshire from Canada. He shakes his head.

"It's amazing to me," he says. "The story behind why people do things."

He hands me a postcard. Advertising an Elvis concert.

"That's me," he says, pointing proudly. "Come and see me."

He tells me that his club would be far and away the best deal for me. Three hundred and twenty pounds as an overseas member. I have just played a round which in itself is a blessing in February for a golfer from Canada, where the courses are shut down from October to April, and my club there, the cheapest private club in Toronto, cost me around six thousand Canadian dollars a year. I have enjoyed it. From the fourth to the seventh hole, the view of the sea is stunning, a spot where J.M.W. Turner painted Scarborough.

My golfing opponent, a barrel-chested canine security man at the RAF Fylingdales listening station, offers this insight on the long par five fifth alongside the North Sea.

"The Americans have moved in," he says, ominously.

I ask what breed of dog he has.

"Belgian Malinois."

His playing partner, a wiry, intense man with short white hair, wearing blue-checkered seersucker pants, seems scruffy and chaotic, but strikes the ball with unerring crispness.

"I almost played hockey for England," he says. "First division, until I was fifty-one."

I can see he has the wrists, the late hit even in his late sixties.

The third man, my partner, Frank, is in his seventies and tells me he has had a triple bypass. Clearly, once an excellent golfer restricted now by health problems and age.

"I spent forty years working in a business for women with seventeen women employees. I had to take an anti-depressant every morning. When I retired, I stopped taking them."

I am thinking he must have had a high-pressure, stressful job in the military or business, and it takes me until the eighteenth fairway to ask the question directly.

"What did you do?"

"Hairdressing. I had a ladies' hairdressing shop. I represented Britain at the World Championship. At one point there were fifty three salons in Scarborough. Seventeen of them were owned by my protégés."

"That's a compliment to you."

"Yes. It were a big deal."

"Did you do those bouffant hairdos in the '60s, the beehive things?"

"Oh yes. Those were my favourite."

"Annette Funicello?"

"Exactly."

A committee member and former President of the Club, he is preoccupied with an upcoming emergency general meeting which is to decide on the firing of Tony the professional. The Elvis Impersonator who lost interest in golf. Although once the holder of five British county championships and the pro since 2000, he suddenly stopped playing golf entirely. I intend to find out why.

There's also some unhappiness with the percentage he is taking from sales in the pro shop, but I don't pry.

After golf, I head down to the legendary Scarborough Cricket Club, which I have read about. It's a heavenly green sward settled down amid blocks of flats and Victorian rooming houses. A match is underway, the batting side is 215 for three. One batsman is 98 not out. I sit in the empty stand and watch. There are perhaps eight spectators.

Three of them walk by. They advise me, the Canadian visitor, on who is playing.

"Scarborough against Stamford Bridge."

The dominant batsman hits a ball firmly wide of midwicket for two, and his hundred. His teammates in the pavilion make a fuss. He skies the next ball, but is dropped. Then forty five overs are done, and the players come off for tea.

To the three I say, "I grew up in South Africa, playing the game, but spent my adult life in Canada. I so missed the culture of cricket."

The helpful trio suggest I go to the bar in the pavilion.

"You'll find a couple of old codgers there who will be happy to talk cricket all day."

I go over, buy a cappuccino from the young lady behind the bar, and settle next to one of the seated men in front of the big windows looking onto the field. I take out the newspaper, the Saturday Guardian. The election is underway and there's lots to read about. But the man abruptly stands up and moves down to a chair at the far end. Odd? Brexit? I am put in mind of a disparaging remark I read in a tabloid about 'latte-sipping Guardian Liberals'. Guilty.

The players troop in for tea. The cricket tea. That civilised British pastime, or wherever the game is played. Tea. The last player to climb up the stairs is the Centurion. I want to catch his eye, express my appreciation, but only if he glances my way.

He does. I nod. The man is tired and acknowledges without enthusiasm. In cricketing terms I can see he is old. Probably in his early thirties, a batsman with some talent who has not quite made it to the County, professional level. He has those three lines emanating from the sides of his eyes, laugh/worry lines.

For every century, there are many failures. And failure in a long batting career can wear a man down. 'Out' is so sudden, so final, irretrievable. A guillotine. Click. You're dead and gone.

After thirty minutes, after some good Guardian reading, the umpires and fielding side take the field. As I descend the stairs I almost bump into the openers. They are kitted out professionally. The pads, the gloves, arm protectors, the helmets. In the days before protective gear, I had been an opener. I know the nerves, the expectation, the optimism tempered by the Damoclean blade. Someone shouts, "Good start, Burnsie." One lefty, one righty, looking downwards as they trot down, doing a little dance-canter over the boundary rope, side-striding over the finely mown outfield towards the pitch, spinning their bats, phantom-forwarding towards the bowlers and fielders warming up.

I want to sit behind the bowler's arm to spot the swing.

There is no more absorbing moment in cricket than the first over or two with the new ball. I love swing, the nick, the flashing chance for the slips. The opening bowler seems very small and young, but he has tremendous whip to his action.

Oddly, I notice, his captain gives him only one slip and sets a very defensive field. The right hander leaves the first ball which swings away late, prods the second square to point off the outside half of his bat and drives at the third, which flies waist height through where a second slip should have been. The ball just rolls over the boundary rope to my right. The first four of the innings. Streaky.

The bowling is good, and the batting quite aggressive. It is good cricket, but no one is there to see it. What keeps these men, and boys, playing? Then I remember my own son's hockey games in Canada, twentysomethings skating and scoring in empty rinks. The thrill, the skill, unobserved.

I decide to leave, taking the long, slow walk around. A fielder patrols the midwicket boundary, and I ask him about the diminutive opening bowler.

"How old is that kid?"

"Ohh… fifteen."

"He's very good."

"Aye, he's useful."

"Very young though, no?"

"Yes."

The fielder, a dark haired young man with a tentative

beard walks in as the bowler from the other end delivers, also a good ball, rearing slightly.

"And how old is he?"

"Sixteen."

We watch a couple more balls.

"The kid from the other end. What's his name?"

"Snowball. Dave."

"Dave Snowball," I say, and, "I'm from Canada. That's a very appropriate name."

I remember Geoff Boycott saying he played his last professional game at Scarborough. When it was over, he walked slowly around the whole field and decided, after more than twenty tumultuous years as one of the greatest, both loved and loathed batsmen in the game, to quit.

I try to imagine what must have gone through his mind, here, as he took his final walk. Looking at this field, at the grass beneath his feet, the curved redbrick gutters, the skies above, all the small dwelling places around him.

As I walk, I realise the next fielder in front of me is Snowball, the kid bowler.

Out in the middle, the batsman drives hard, the ball hitting the non-striking batsman on the hip. He yelps and drops in pain.

"Good fielder, that batsman," I crack.

"Yeah," Snowball laughs.

He has a thin, slightly spotty face, with hair that sticks up like a cockscomb, still the face of a boy.

"You were unlucky."

He chuckles.

"Your skipper should have given you a second slip in your first over, new ball moving away and all."

"Oh well," he says shyly, scuffing the grass with his toe. Not his position to criticise, publicly anyway.

"You're very good."

"Thanks."

The injured batsman is getting some attention. It isn't serious. There's laughter.

"How fast do you bowl?"

"About seventy."

"Not bad."

The struck batsman is back on his feet, his partner patting the pitch with his bat as if keen to get on with it.

"You must eat lots of bacon, potatoes and pasta to build up enough weight to open for Yorkshire, eh?" The Canadian, eh.

The boy nods as I move off past a woman in the stands with a brown Labrador and a big-lensed camera.

"You're the official photographer, are you?" I say.

"No," she laughs, nodding towards the pitch. "I've got a son out there."

A sonn, said the Yorkshire way.

Maybe there's a grandpa who cannot come who will love to see the pictures.

Speaking of Geoff Boycott, he is giving a talk at the Scarborough Spa, a seafront entertainment complex in that resort town. I get a ticket that enables me to join him for a meet and greet before his speech.

When I was a thirteen year old boy in South Africa, just falling in love with cricket, I went to my first test match at the Wanderers with my friend Robert Lister.

The great MCC team is playing my beloved Springboks.

Our tearaway opening bowler Peter Pollock is pawing the ground at the Golf Club End. England's new opening batsman Geoff Boycott, with his glasses, and skinny, meticulous manner looks like a bank clerk, but he is from Yorkshire, and this means something. Len Hutton, Brian Close, Ray Illingworth, Freddie Trueman. Tough, adversarial fighters who will hurt you to win. Quite the opposite of the effete, snobbish players foreigners often associate with English cricketers.

In his first over, Pollock delivers a rocket, Boycott fends at it, there's a loud click and wicketkeeper Denis Lindsay and the slips roar in unison. People in faraway Bloemfontein probably hear the click. But the thin bespectacled man stands his ground. There's a momentary stunned silence, the beginnings of an angry rumble in the crowd, and then the roar as the umpire lifts his finger.

When I meet Boycott, I tell him this story. He avoids eye contact. The skin on his cheek, burned by so many years in the sun, has a snake-like sheen.

"And you walked back to the tunnel at the Wanderers in such a way, slowly, shaking your head, that you almost had me convinced that you didn't touch it." I deliver this with a grudgingly respectful air.

After all, here is a man who, after that dismissal, went on to score a hundred and several fifties in that series and ultimately onwards to become one of the most respected and prolific openers in the history of the game.

"I didn't hit it," he insists, with conviction. "You've got it all wrong."

He is clearly annoyed.

"I don't know where you get your facts, but I never hit it. "

He is determined to correct me, all these years later.

"In fact, I got 48."

Later in the drinks session, he comes back to me and says, "Y'know Barlow admitted he touched that ball that he wasn't given out for, in the fifth test at Newlands. So others were doing that!"

And he nods at me. Case closed.

Later I look it up, and there it is.

Boycott c Lindsay b Pollock P 4

Later the crowd packs into the auditorium and grey-haired Yorkshire folk, a few with sons and grandsons, hang on his every word. He is brilliant. I am reminded of something Brian Mulroney, the Conservative Prime Minister of Canada, once said. "Walking into a room full of Tories is like stepping into a warm bath." Same with Boycs, I bet.

A grizzled man sitting next to me, with the slight whiff of ale on his breath, tells me he loves Boycott.

"'E's my hero. I saw his 100th century at Headingley. A real fighter."

I tell him about the Wanderers incident.

He chuckles. "Ooh, Boycs *never* walked," said with admiration.

Although Boycott infuriates many, and women distrust him because of an assault case brought by an ex-girlfriend, this crowd attests to those who say he is the Greatest Living Yorkshireman.

Here, he can do no wrong.

MONDAY 8TH MAY

MY NAME IS DROGO DE LA BEAUVRIÉRE

I decide to explore a part of North Yorkshire I haven't yet been to. Namely the south-east quadrant. That will take me eventually to the sea, so I consult the map and choose Skipsea. Turns out Skipsea has a castle. So off I go in my red Vauxhall. Thirty minutes or so later I nearly miss the turnoff. I have a half empty bottle of water. A nice lady in the village with three spaniels fills it up.

"Do you want some fruit juice?" she asks.

"No. Just water, please."

While I talk to and play with her little cocker spaniels, she disappears around the back of her house.

She returns with the full container.

"You should find it very cold."

"Why, thank you," I say. "Lovely dogs."

"Thank you," she says.

Skipsea Castle turns out to be not much more than a big green mound and a plaque. Apparently, in the eleventh century, the victorious invader William the Conqueror gives a castle to a French noble with a very long name. Here it is:

"He gave it to Drogo de la Beauvriére, who had fought alongside him at the Battle of Hastings in 1066. The king needed a trusted follower there to control the area and the adjacent coastline."

Drogo de la Beauvrière. What a moniker. My kids and I used to joke about the line in The Princess Bride, "My name is Inigo Montoya. Chew killed my father. Prepare to die."

I see him with peaked cap, moustache and long black wavy hair.

"My name is Drogo de la Beauvriére. You killed my father. Prepare to die."

I have to walk through a small herd of cows, avoiding their runny patties of poo, covered in bluebottle flies. One calf butts aggressively at his mama's teats. I climb up the grass-covered mound and look around, three sixty. Farms and fields, woods and villages. I descend but the footpath leads nowhere in particular, so I decide to walk around the field and return to the car. The edge of the field runs up to and below a wold, or wood. A sudden movement, ahead of me, about eighty yards away draws the eye. A small buck-like creature breaks from cover and springs into the trees. It isn't a deer. Too thickset and short for that. It has thick fur and a broad back, but is lower to the ground than a deer. It isn't a wild pig. I think it is a rare sighting, but take it no further. Watching it though, a thought occurs. It is as alive as you and I, now, at this instant, its heart beating with the instincts of fear and refuge.

I drive on further, following my GPS to Skipsea. The road on the digital map goes past a sign in real life which says No Entry, Dangerous Erosion. I drive through, drawn to the danger. Sure enough, like some surrealist painting, the road goes to the end of a low cliff and… disappears, into the sea, over the horizon, quite perfectly. Another man following me in a white van gets out and passes me as I gather my things, my water, my energy bar, my iPod and my walking stick, and I say to him, I say, "It's the end of the world."

And he grunts, "So it is", and smiles ever so slightly. He walks to the end of the road, to the end of the world, stands for a while taking in the 180 degree view of the North Sea, and heads back to his van.

I walk along the cliff a while. There's a slight onshore breeze, the tide is low, white horses ride in on the wave tops for miles around. I drop down onto the sands. I walk and walk. I listen to my music. I eventually stop a shuffle of David Bowie, The Stones, Dylan, Hank Williams and Beethoven and listen just to Van Morrison.

After all a while, my brain starts to fire. I start having all sorts of creative thoughts. Snatches of Van's lyric about a Robin prompt this. Every time he sees a Robin it makes him want to sing. I think of my daughter, Tess. She wants to sing when loved ones are around. A Great Joy. Far ahead I see a lonely pier jutting out to sea, covered in the green algae of a thousand tides. This is my aim point, my destination. There's one in every walk.

I see old men with young men near the waveline. A father and son. You can tell by the similarity of their bent backs. They're digging for something, with pipes sucking up the mud, hard on their backs, I think, like fruitpickers, always bent over, not what God intended for the human body, bent over like that for hours.

To my left, just above the line of the crumbling clay brown cliffs, the roofs of caravans. Further on in a country field, an old concrete bunker. After an hour, I reach the pier but it is carpeted in green slime. I turn around, clambering up the rocks to a path back along the clifftop.

The bunker turns out to be a wartime gun emplacement[1]. I go in. It looks and smells like winos have been living there for years, mattress on the ground, squashed cans and packets lying around. The little slits in the walls are perfectly angled so each one gives a defender with a gun coverage of about three hundred yards along the shoreline. I get an echo in the blood. A sense of forefathers defending this island realm. How local Yorkshiremen must have manned these emplacements in anticipation of a seaborne German invasion that never came. Then I recall something I'd read somewhere that militarily the German High Commands favoured land

[1] As it turns out, I find on the internet the Pillbox Study Group and these are Pillbox Type 22, not described as gun emplacements, set up in the Second World War at many sites, including North Yorkshire.

clashes, and air bombardment, but they did not favour or become expert at seaborne invasions.

My walk back is through the caravan parks waiting for the summer invasion and another generation of broken hearts and scratched knees.

I listen to Jane Eyre and Frederick Forsyth's life story, The Outsider, but it is an Everly Brothers song that seems appropriate to the caravans-in-waiting. *How can I meet her…?*

SATURDAY 13TH MAY

THE GARLIC CARPET

Compared to North America, the newspapers and television here are fantastic. There's at least one thing worth watching every night, often three. Every morning, with coffee, four of the newspapers are worth an hour's reading. The issues are big. The future of Britain in Europe, eruptions of terrorism, refugee crises, and the bizarre and volatile Trump.

On Saturday I see a program on the Yorkshire Wolds. It's interesting that in the heart of prime time there are quality programmes about nature in Britain.

In the Wolds show, some yappy fit chap is walking the Wold Way having an explore, here and there.

In one village, Nunburnholme, he goes to the local church. In the second half of the 19th century the vicar is Francis Orpen-Morris.

He is the author of definitive books on Britain's Birds, Butterflies and Moths.

After watching the programme, I google Nunburnholme. It's thirty five minutes away. I find out there's a church service there at ten forty five. I plan on getting there for that, then walking the Yorkshire Wold Way for a couple of hours. Maybe after all these years away from Him, God will put an added spring in my step.

It's a typical, beautiful old stone church in a green graveyard. There's a tombstone for a nineteen year old private from the First World War. I stand before it and wonder if, from some awful trench, he yearned for the peace and beauty of this piece of heaven.

Nineteen.

Inside, a small lady is showing a young couple the church. I stand back until they are finished. The couple has recently moved from Leeds to York, are engaged, and are looking for a place to get married. He must be six feet eight, and says not a word. His fiancée is barely five foot tall and does all the talking.

When they are done and the couple has left, he, bending over to exit the ancient doorway, I ask the church lady about last night's TV show; but she didn't see it.

"Oh, it was very good. The priest here, Reverend Orpen-Morris, was described as one of Britain's great naturalists."

"No, I didn't see it," she repeats.

I change the subject.

"I plan to walk the Wold Way but I forgot to fill my water bottle. Is there any water in the church?"

She reaches for the bottle. No, there isn't but she will go home and meet me at the top of the nearby field with my bottle, filled.

I enter the Wold Way in the sheep field across the lane and when I get to the top there she is, with my bottle, and a second.

"That's very kind of you," I say.

I follow the Way up a steep hill through a wood above the village. A dirt path leads off into it, to my right. I stop. Then proceed. Then stop, go back. Something about the path beckons. Soon I see why. A short way in, the wood is brilliantly carpeted with white flowers, thick with them. They reflect a light breaking through the trees off the floor illuminating the whole scene. It's magical. Rev Orpen-Morris must have walked here and seen this very sight some hundred and twenty years before. There are also patches of bluebells. I emerge above the village and drop down to the road through somebody's back yard, and past a sign that says CHIEN FURIEUX. I wander around the village, as I am still an hour short of my minimum two hour walk, and eventually find a wooden sign that says Yorkshire Wold Way. I follow it across a field which ends in a concrete drive deeply covered by water. I head to the right and find the stream narrows, pick a spot and wade across, finding myself in a thorn hedge facing a barbed wire fence. I force myself through, getting torn by thorns and stung by nettles, but those stings only last about eight hours and are superficial. I strike out up a field to the crest of a hill where I find another marked stile leading nowhere. My inner compass nudges me westwards. I pass the carcass of what looks like a hawk, its body flensed of flesh, its wings still intact. I am listening to Richard Ford's The Death of Others and I can see what his readers get excited about. The previous five stories are okay, if you like dark middle class ageing American male cynicism, but 'Death' holds my attention.

I eventually come upon a well-worn farmer's track, which leads to a road, which leads me back down to Nunburnholme village, and a bench in a park, where I stop for my sandwich.

There's another couple in the park. I approach them.

"Are you from around here?" I ask.

"Yes, we are."

"Oh. The reason I ask is I have just walked through the most amazing carpet of wild flowers in that wood there."

"What did they look like?"

"Brilliant white."

"Wild garlic. They come out for a few days this time of year."

MONDAY 15TH MAY

NETTLED IN OULSTON

I wake this morning feeling blah. I'd had a dream about a former colleague who's become a successful novelist. He is locked in a glassed-in booth, at the YMCA, writing furiously. I want to say hi to him but I am told Mr Linden Macintyre cannot be disturbed.

I find myself in the caravan, alone, a long way from my family. Am I wasting precious time being away from them? I feel rather useless, unmoored in Toronto now I've shut down my filmmaking business after a couple of setbacks. I'd had enough. I've always loved the feeling of quitting, of walking away from things. It's been a recurring urge in my life. South Africa and apartheid: The CBC and corporate journalism: a job I once had delivering magazines. I just walked away for that thrill of freedom.

To get myself back to normal I do a longer session of Pilates, then have fruit and egg and bacon. Then I prepare the pheasant in port for George and Jools' farewell dinner tomorrow night. Crush six Juniper berries. I fashion a crusher out of the heavy egg cup I bought in a charity shop and the handle of the sieve spoon. Chopped onions and garlics. Salt and pepper. Put the two pheasant, the brace, into the crockpot and pour the port in.

Then I take Geoff Brooks' Howardien Hills walking book, close my eyes and pick a walk. Oulston.

I drive about ten miles, through Hovingham, where I stop for a cappuccino and newspaper. At Oulston, as I follow the directions out of the village, I bump into a man with an affectionate Labrador and checked cloth cap. It's raining slightly.

"No umbrella?" I say.

"No. I'm not bothered," he barks toughly.

It's a great two-hour walk. I have another encounter with nettles. I'd downloaded some Beatles; then I listen to a big chunk of Frederick Forsyth's autobiography, about getting fired by the BBC on his first foreign assignment to Biafra. Then he went back in, *on his own coin.* That separates the true correspondent from the hacks.

I follow the directions and a public footpath into a farm property that has a contradictory sign that says Private: Do Not Enter. A lanky farmer is crossing a field towards me. Could have been anywhere between thirty and fifty. He seems stressed and languid at the same time.

"I hope I'm not trespassing," I say.

"No. No, not at all."

We consult over my little book, and he points me on my way.

"May I ask a question?"

He nods, a little wary now.

"Are most of the farms family-owned around here?"

"Most of them were, like this one. Fourth generation. But they are dying out, especially the small ones. Big agribusiness, lots of hectares is the trend."

He looks a bit Clint Eastwood-ish with deep creases in his cheeks. Older than his age, I suspect.

"What do you farm?" I ask.

"Pigs, arable and sheep."

"Thanks."

He points at a kissing gate across his field.

"That way. Then aim for that big tree, and Low Farm across there."

I can see the roof.

I switch to Jane Eyre. A story, it seems, of a servant woman's crush on her employer. Despite his direction, I lose my bearings a bit and have another tussle with Yorkshire stinging nettles. The rain comes down, and I am slowed by mud but eventually guess right and re-emerge at Oulston, two hours on.

My appetite is up, and I shall sleep like a log.

I speak to my son Griffin, the poker pro, who is back in London, but leaving for Vegas in a couple of weeks. My dear friend Henri is coming to visit.

I pick some flowers and jam them into a letter to Nicky.

TUESDAY 16TH MAY

FERRY TO BELFAST

I decide to leave Castle Howard for a quick tour of Northern Ireland, and Ireland, before Nicky gets here. Always wanted to visit Belfast. Intend to do the Van Morrison walk tomorrow, check out The Falls Road. Staying in 'Laura's B and B' for twenty seven quid a night. Am somewhat shocked to discover that the return trip on the ferry (returning overnight Monday Dublin-Liverpool) costs three hundred and four pounds. Yikes.

Got into the wine and port a bit, but hit the road early for the four plus hour drive to the ferry port in West Scotland, Cairnryan. Started out in rain, but last hour is sunlight and scudding clouds.

Drive past Southwick but don't visit. I think things might have played themselves out. My sister, Ann, had married David, the son of that house many years ago, but it ended in a terrible tragedy. David's sister is a special woman. I visualise her now, somewhere over my right shoulder. She sits next to an Aga cooker in a large kitchen, reading next to a window with a breathtaking view of Scottish valleys. I had found some letters from David and had sent them to her. At first she seemed happy, but then had second thoughts, evoking an unhappy recollection.

Stirring memories over a life gone, a sadness that will never go away. How does one deal with this near the end of one's life? David lies in the local graveyard with his son and my nephew Rupert, and their names, the last time I was there, are worn away, barely visible. Barely a handful remember their laughing red-haired ways.

On the ferry, much larger than I expect, we are passing the Isle of Arran to starboard and a lighthouse point to port. The trip takes close to three hours. The sun is out. Beautiful sailing conditions. Northern Ireland, here I come.

WEDNESDAY 17TH MAY

NO TORIES NO BREXIT NO BORDER

In a B and B room in a house all to myself. It's very quiet. I leave my meds in Yorkshire so have to find some here. A pharmacist tells me of a doctor who will see me. Dr Thomson of Forster Green comes through. A bashful, scruffy, open-necked shirt kind of guy, very informal. I suspect he has worked in far-off places. They cost me three pounds ten pence.

Belfast seems unexpectedly ordinary. I walk for miles up Ormeau Road to the hospital and at one point stroll next to a government IT guy with a very strong accent.

"They'll never solve things here," he says, in response to my questioning, waiting for the light to turn green. "Though there is a peace, for now."

More election signs here than in Northern England. He explains that Sinn Fein, though it has some MPs at Westminster, doesn't sit. They still get paid and apparently donate most of their salaries to their community.

Northern Ireland wants to stay in the EU. It makes their border with Ireland in the south melt away. Now there are fears the border will rise again.

It's as if any unexpected jolt will upset the whole delicate peace.

I like Sein Fein's election poster.

NO TORIES

NO BORDER

NO BREXIT

I eat dinner at a pub. The softest bangers and mash with a delicious gravy, and a shandy. Right in front of me, for a long time, a tattooed man fiercely kisses his gypsy lover. Never seen that in an English pub. He is built like a tank, is bald as a tick, heavily muscled and has shiny blue eyes. He notices me, and seems to zero in, staring. I look down. I have an instinct I won't enjoy his suspicions of where I'm from. Hard man. I've read about those someplace.

Tomorrow I walk the Van Morrison trail.

Playing Royal County Down on Sunday.

Being here is strange in a nice, isolated, anonymous and unpressured way. The soft adventures of a retired sixty six-year old peripatetic.

Tired.

THURSDAY 18TH MAY

UP ON CYPRUS AVENUE

In my imagination I'd somehow assumed Belfast to be a wild place, a hotbed of creativity seething with political rage.

I walk for four hours through Van Morrison's Belfast and come away with a different impression. It's square. Lots of little unremarkable boxes in clean residential blocks.

There are tight, poorer streets with two-story houses jammed together, attached on both sides. One of those is Hyndford Street. Like many communities in Britain, or at least in Yorkshire, the houses are clearly lived in, cars are parked outside them, the little front gardens show hard work and neatness, gardens and rocks and fountains and flowering bushes and clipped hedges. But there are no people. At least no people to be seen, unless scurrying from car-to-door, from door-to-car. One senses they are all watching from behind the windows, but one sees nobody. It's odd. Perhaps during the day they get on their phones and call their friends who are also inside watching the street. And they talk about what they see.

"Ida?"

"Yes, dear."

"There's a fella on the street."

"Aye?"

"Large. Lookin' about."

"At Van's place?"

"Yet another."

"He never really lived here, after a boy, y'know."

"You told me, Soph."

"Couldn't wait to get out of here, if you ask me."

125 Hyndford, where Morrison grew up, is a fifteen minute walk to the docks where his dad worked. The exterior is in perfect condition with a tasteful plaque donated by the Belfast Blues Appreciation Society. I look them up on my cellphone but the plaque seems to be the only thing they've done.

Five minutes away is Elmgrove Primary School, a moderately sized, handsome, old red-brick building. Just a schoolboy's run away is The Hollow, as in 'Down in the hollow... you brown-eyed girl.'

Here the Connswater River flows, nothing more than a large stream really. There's a stone bridge, sheltered by trees. One can imagine the lad sporting with his girls here in times past.

Two minutes away on Greenville Street, I read that Van would grab lunch at a bakery whilst Cleaning Windows, when he was playing in skiffle and early blues bands before Them and the hits started to flow.

He used to, he has said, go up the hill some twenty minutes to "a whole different universe", Cyprus Avenue. It's a much wider street than Hyndford, framed by beautiful arching trees and wide pavements in front of very substantial houses, belonging, one assumes, to the moneyed men of Belfast, lawyers, doctors and the like. As one turns into Cyprus from busy Beersbridge Road, peace and quiet embrace. Save for the sweet birdsong and the lyrics in my head.

At the top of Cyprus Avenue, four schoolchildren wait for the bus, animated, laughing. Two boys, two girls. I ask them if they are from Van's high school, Orangefield. A girl who looks like Lady Gaga in a convent uniform, with eruptive white hair and a joyously beautiful bounce in her accent and voice says the name of her school, Saint Mary's or St someone else, and says, I sense with nose up and finger turned down somewhat, no no no Orangefield, that's down the hill and across the park.

Down the Hill
and across the Park
the scruffy boys
dream and dwell
and look longingly
at you
a shocking goddess
click-clacking of the high heeled shoes

Van Morrison went there I say
and they look at me
smiling
but agape
a silvering old man
with a funny accent
mumbling about
Van Who?
A ghost, maybe
Some hero in
His head.

Cyprus Avenue represents a yearning, a promised land, I'm thinking. Lennon, Presley, Morrison, none were immune from reaching for love across class lines; some put flowers on their new Rolls and strayed from wives for women with fancy names and toffee in their cheeks.

On the descent into Orangefield, a park like many other urban parks I have walked in Canada or South Africa too, with hidden footways to dirty urban streams, plastic bags and things in the mud, and beyond the park, the identical roofs. The uniformity of the boxes conveys suffocation, conformity of some specific and unique velocity stuffed down the throat, amounting to the fierce shaping of no-risk civilian battalions, getting up and down in their own way, day in and day out, saluting and obeying, dying for the flag that controls their neighbourhood. And this in a city that has such blood-filled combustion in its history, and even now. The radio news announcer says sectarian murders are Up. Up? Who knew? I thought it was over? Why now? Here Orangefield is signposted on a Union Jack and the murals are of brave Ulstermen of yore, how many died in WW1, here, there and every Imperial everywhere. I still don't understand how 'Sir' Van fits into the Troubles. He must have transcended and escaped them.

I stop for something to eat. A harried thin-faced woman behind the deli counter twitches irritably when I hand back her menu and say I want nothing with bread, and though it's not on the menu, could I please just have soup and salad. She nods, mutely. I sit and wait on a stool at the window beside a table with the only other customers. They are a hugely obese family of five. The father, whose posture screams out, to me, don't look, don't stare. He must be three hundred pounds plus and two severely overweight daughters. It's two in the afternoon and they are doggedly consuming mounded plates of chips and eggs and bacon and potatoes smeared with sauce. It's like slow-motion family suicide, I think.

She brings me a sluggish soup of indeterminate provenance but a wonderful salad. When I go to pay, I wait behind a tall handsome man in paint-spattered torn overalls, the window cleaner, or roofer. I leave her a big tip, for some reason, sharing her sorrows.

From Orangefield to Ormeau Park, I have a thought. So Van Morrison is a lad born with a rampant, raging imagination, a lyrical genius, and a Celtic soul ignited by

Radio Luxembourg and black American blues crackling through the rainy nights. It transports him and he escapes, escapes this place of brain-boxing boxes. All the box houses, the stentorian religions, the rage turned inward.

Isn't so much great art born out of such fury? Great Art must by definition tear down the artifice, yet the artifice, nourished by obedience of the fearful, outlives all the singers and painters and writers of the ages.

Somewhere I read Morrison said that to be great you have to be the greatest son of a bitch of all. I remember a story a musician friend told me. When Jeff Healy, the blind Canadian virtuoso guitarist, plays Montreux, Van is there. A meeting is arranged. Van is very plastered. When he is introduced to Healy, he pauses, looks at him, spits in his face, and walks away. I find it hard to believe, but my friend was there, and I see no reason in him to make this up.

Morrison's mother Violet died. There's a newspaper picture of him following her casket out of the church. His face is pale and, to my eye, pulled back with grief. He's been crying, as a man should in those circumstances.

So he is able to get away, far far far away. And now he can come back, to honour a mother who was a tireless church singer. An old man now who immortalised the rebellions that enable him to survive this Belfast town.

That's my guess anyway.

FRIDAY 19TH MAY

THE DOWNPATRICK RACES

If there's heaven on earth on days like this it may be in Northern Ireland. I wake to sunshine in Belfast and walk to a nearby cafe for cappuccino and the Guardian. It is packed with broken-nosed, head shaven labourers being served by two hair-dyed forty year olds, ex-hot chicks, the Irish equivalent of hardass broads tightly clad in leather and spandex. Maybe it's a sisters kitchen.

I don't fit in but they are very friendly. Cappuccino clearly isn't in their repertoire, but what they serve up is hot and strong, with a crest of what looks and tastes like shaving cream from a canister of some kind.

Then the drive up the hill, leaving Belfast to Downpatrick. I'm playing the world's Number One rated golf course, Royal County Down on Sunday, so need to find my swing at an easier course. Just enter golf course on googlemaps and go to the closest flag. Downpatrick. Eighteen holes for thirty quid.

It's on the way to my B and B in Newcastle. Arrive just before noon and check in with the guy I think is the pro but he tells me he's just the IT man fixing their computer system. Still, he takes my dough and walks me to the first tee.

"It's a hilly track, and the greens are very good. The pros come and practise on them before playing tournaments at RCD. They are pretty much the same."

He gestures at the first tee.

"Will you be going to the races?"

"What races?"

"Oh, you've gotta go to the races. There's Friday night racing at five. On the way to Newcastle just out of town, on your left. You can't miss it. It's a treat when the weather's this fine."

Turns out I have the golf course entirely to myself. At one point I see one other golfer, briefly, riding along in some kind of motorised chariot, standing, his clubs lashed on behind. He is there and gone like a Ben Hur comic turn. It *is* quite hilly, the kind of walk that puts that nice strain on the hamstrings, and at its highest point offers a breathtaking 360 degree view of Northern Ireland. The ocean in the distance off to the right, lakes to the left, farm fields forever, the town of Downpatrick with two magnificent church steeples, one of them apparently containing the Tomb of Saint Patrick himself. I hold the moment as long as I can. I feel like spinning around and around and around like Julie Andrews in the Sound of Music.

The tee I am on, number seven, drops off way down below, and there is a following breeze. At the bottom of the valley, a wood encroaches from the left. A big oak stands about twenty yards in from the out-of-bounds hedge on the right. I lay into my drive, just inside the tree with a slight late fade. It lands and kicks hard and big straight on. I walk it off. As I reach the flat part of the fairway I see my ball, on the fairway in perfect position, 140 yards out. With bounce and the following wind it's 328 yards. For some reason I kiss the tips of my two right fingers and raise them to the sky. I am thanking the Almighty (whatever one calls Him or Her) for letting me live long enough to feel this moment. A golfer's apogee, at sixty six. Such is my absorption with this game, and the concentration I welcome on every shot, the solitary bliss. The round passes in a dreamlike rhythm, and I hit a few more perfect shots. It's an open generous course. One of my favourite, ever. A chance discovery, the best.

When I am finished, I thank the pro.

"Yourself for company?" he says.

"Yeah, I don't mind at all."

"It's a bit off the beaten track. Hard to get known."

"Well, I'll pass it on. It's a great deal, a lovely course. I needed to sharpen up. I'm playing Royal County Down on Sunday."

There's a drop in the mood, like atmospheric pressure.

As soon as Royal County Down was out of my mouth, a tousled boy sitting opposite him snaps his eyes at me, as if I was in Cajun country and had announced I was going to take a walk down to Alligator Swamp. The pro looks at me knowingly.

"You'll never have an experience like it, but if I could offer you some advice," says the pro, "don't even think about your score. It's very very tough."

"Yes. Right now my driving just isn't consistently accurate enough."

They are just like all the locals who shake their heads when I say I'm playing it.

"It'll beat you up," says the computer man.

The boy shakes his head.

I buy a Caesar salad at the local grocery store, Lidl.

I take it to the cafe at the bus station. Two schoolgirls are perched on a stool and one says to me, as I exit with my cappuccino.

"*Who* are you, man?"

I'm so surprised I don't respond, and set up outside, watching all the high school kids making their buses home. Uniforms, knapsacks, earplugs. What awaits them?

On the way out of town, I see the sign to the Downpatrick race track and turn in. It's quite what one would imagine. Park in a cow field. A circle of bookies standing in front of computerised stakes boards, and terminals, yelling out names of racetracks everywhere and starting times. "Aintree, five thirty."

I chat up a bookie called Ed, who tells me he's retired. He's just setting up.

“ ’Cept people keep calling me up offering me money, so here I am.”

Ed has a clean face, a sharp beak, and narrow glittering eyes. Lots of smile lines around his eyes and mouth, tanned. You just feel he must have had a happy life.

“I’m from Canada. Never been to an Irish horserace in my life. You got a tip for me, Ed?”

“Number One in the six thirty. So I’m told. But you never really know. It’s a mug’s game.”

“My sister always said if you don’t know what you’re doing, and I don’t have a clue, bet the second favourite.”

“Not a bad plan,” says Ed.

The second favourite in the first race is Cajun Sam at 7/2.

“Give me a fiver, each way, would ya?”

He gives me the slip which says I shall win thirty three pounds if she wins, eight if she places.

It’s a helluva course. I’ve never seen anything like it. Deep green grass, winding in a long oblong shape, over hill and dale, out of sight down into a gully on the other side, then up so you can see the horses’ silhouettes against the distant sky, and low brush fences all the way around.

My jockey has green and yellow colours and a yellow cap. The first time around, and in front of us spectators, the jockeys are composed on their galloping horses, beautifully balanced, up in their stirrups, conserving energies, reins taut, knees slightly bent, holding positions. The horses look like they have a lot in reserve, and the sound of their flying hooves is exhilarating, the rumble from them drumming through my chest.

I look around at all the Irish faces, completely attentive. Lots of couples on dates, the girls dressed to the nines. Heels, gold lame, lots of hair product and lots of make-up, their young men in sharp black suits, white shirts, black narrow ties and dark glasses. Old men with craggy lines and flat caps.

Cajun Sam holds sixth all the way around, the second long meandering, rolling lap. There's a large TV screen alongside me.

The pack ghosts across the far horizon, almost disappears except for the bobbing, speeding caps, then re-appears, heading downhill for the last jump, appreciably faster, spreading out a bit as the laggers drop off and the leaders surge. Cajun Sam is moving up, now fifth, now fourth, now over the jump and lands and drops. The jockey goes over his ears in a face plant.

He's down!

I can't believe it. The following horse veers and throws its jockey, falling sickeningly into the inner rail which collapses like a large hose. It lies on the ground, shuddering. I look around expecting people to look as horrified as I feel, expecting someone to do something, but of course the crowd stays with the winners only. The remaining horses are now going as hard as they can. Their jockeys are driving them on, but only one seems to have his crop out, thrashing wildly. People cry out, "Go… Charge… C-maaan." The winners blow by it seems just a few feet from us, now sweating, the jockeys mud-spattered, their faces red with exertion. Somebody else wins obviously, and out there where my horse and rider fell there is already a knot of officials, vets, emergency vehicles and the race ambulance.

I quick stride over to Ed.

"Ed, my horse went down."

"I know. I was thinking of you."

"He was doing great."

"He would've been in the money, the way he was coming on."

"Is he alright?"

"What do you mean?"

"Injured? Put down?"

"Oh, I don't know. They don't say. You'll have to ask around."

I pass on the next race. It's only four horses.

The only other time I go to the races, with my sister, who was a competitive point-to-point rider, was in the 1960s in Salisbury, Rhodesia. She picks two winners for my father just by looking at how the horses behave in the warm-up ring.

So for the third race, the six thirty, I decide to bet a tenner each way on Ed's tip, number #1, who happens also to be second favourite, and pick a second one, in honour of my sister, who looks spicy in the ring. Five pounds each way on number 12.

#12. A big horse giving its handler all she can take.

Capucco Sox, in the purple silks. One of my favourite colours, too. He is eyeing the course like he can't wait to get out there, his ears pricked up tight. I go back to Ed.

He does a bit of a double take at Capucco Sox. There it is at the bottom of his list. 20-1.

"He looks real good in the ring," I say, faux-knowingly.

"Best o'luck," he says as I examine my ticket. "But remember. It's a mug's game."

Wow. I could win a hundred and thirty seven pounds if Capucco comes in. That will pay for all my B and Bs on this trip.

They both start well and for two-thirds of the race are in the leading clump. But neither horse finishes. Somewhere out there they drop out.

I call it quits and say goodbye to racing in Northern Ireland. But what a day out. For the people. Cloudless. Blinding blue, and blinding green and galloping colours, money lost, money made.

Now I sit in my Airbnb down the coast past Newcastle, with a view of the Irish sea, and a cup of Rooibos. I shall finish off that Caesar salad, watch a bit of golf and crash.

It's almost nine pm. There's still not a cloud in the sky. A truly beautiful day.

SATURDAY 20TH MAY

WHERE'S PETER O'TOOLE WHEN YOU NEED HIM?

Today is an open day. Nothing scheduled or planned. In retirement, not my description of it, there are many more of those than ever before in one's life. One wakes up to an empty canvas. There's nowhere to go. No job. No meetings. No deadlines. This can be intimidating, even depressing. Or like an empty canvas, it can be filled. Or it can fill up by simply moving into it.

In County Down, so I resolve to take a hike in the Mountains of Mourne.

First, breakfast with my B and B hosts, Bryan and Catherine, who have converted a third generation family farmhouse overlooking the sea between Newcastle and Kilkeen into a really pleasant B and B. My room is pin-neat, comfy big bed, fridge with milk, water and chocolate bars, en-suite bathroom, in a separate wing, quiet.

They wait in the kitchen with eight different types of cereal, and broad smiles. They seem a little disappointed when all I choose is a bowl of muesli with some strawberries. And a cup of tea, for which I bring my own Rooibos teabag.

"My boss is South African and will only drink Rooibos," Catherine says, a warm and, may I say, well-endowed schoolteacher in nearby Downpatrick. It's what I notice, what can I say, and it's lovely.

Bryan is a bespectacled, slightly breathless photographer who wears a shirt with a Land Rover logo and the words NI Land Rover Society, est 1996. In the name of asking people about subjects they are comfortable with, I ask about the Land Rover society.

Within three minutes I am regretting this. Land Rovers are his obsession. He is unstoppable and uninterruptible. Like any rabid hobbyist or collector he seems oblivious to the degree of interest I have in Land Rovers. For me, all automobiles are the demon seed of our compulsory fossil fuel addiction, though I do remember, growing up in Africa, how iconic Land Rovers were in the bush, on farms, practical and reassuringly durable. Once in Kenya, me and my documentary crew escaped out of a swampy area in front of a suddenly hostile herd of elephants in a churning, whining four wheel drive Land Rover. I am as grateful for and respectful of Land Rovers as the next traveller. But by the time he is describing the third phase of a Land Rover driving skills competition he judged in County Wicklow and his own wife asks to be excused with an implicit rolling of the eyes, I realise I am going to have to pull a tangential extrication. Interrupting, I say, "It's remarkable how wealthy young people buy these powerful bush vehicles when they never leave the cities. Take for example the Humvee."

It slows him momentarily like a log in front of a flooding river, but he churns on, explaining how he bought his current Range Rover three point oh, V.6 and rechipped it from its urban pre-owner to adapt the vehicle to his own off-road use.

I throw another obstacle in his way. "What's your take on the driverless car?" but I'm doomed.

"Look at this," he says.

He leaps up, dashes across the kitchen and is back, shoving a small container with two chips under my nose like a perfume salesman.

"Cost me four hundred and fourteen pounds, each. Manages everything."

"Wow," I say uncomprehendingly impressed. (Manages? How? Don't.)

In an abrupt attempt to get away, I polish off my muesli in three rapid spoonsful, push my plate aside and say, "That's it for me. Great."

"Do you want a tour of the house?"

Ignoring that, I respond, "Do you have a map of mountain hikes?"

He does.

Then he follows me to the door, and the last thing he says is, "*If you are not back by three, I'll call out the search party.*"

Odd, I think. Me, search party. How ridiculous. How embarrassing. How costly.

Those silly people who cross the Atlantic backwards, blindfolded in a bath tub.

They should pay for the search and rescue and naval costs of five countries to save them.

The Mountains of Mourne are right behind the house, and the little red Vauxhall heads up the narrow stone walled winding road to higher ground. A big Mercedes is tailgating me, in a hurry, so at the first lay by I pull over. I started doing this about three years ago, part of ageing. It's strangely satisfying. One soon catches up to the overtaking car and we both always reach the next stop together. What's the point? But in this case the Mercedes judders to a halt, the window is down and a thin woman shouts over a boy who seems to be her son in the passenger seat and in what strikes me as a Chicago accent says, "Are you from around here?"

"No. I'm Canadian, never been here before in my life," slightly superior.

Window up and she's off. Two hundred yards further along, she judders again to a halt next to a woman walking with her daughter. For five minutes or so, they engage in detailed directions, blissfully unaware that I am stuck behind her. She goes a little further and pulls over. I continue, looking for a road that runs along the bottom of Slieve Donald, which will take me to a walk which starts between Slieve Binion and Slieve Muck. I assume

Slieve means mount. (It does, says Google.) Soon enough she is up my ass again like the truck in 'Duel'.

I repress the instinct to think "damn Americans" to myself. Unsuccessfully, for a second. I 'covered' America from Washington for a spell in the '80s. Trump doesn't surprise me at all. He's an apotheosis.

I take a hairpin bend ahead and the Mercedes thankfully swooshes on.

I am looking for a walk to a high dam which starts in a parking area I never find, but there is the dam between the two sleeves, we'll call them. I pull over and follow an old tar road down towards the water. It's a beautiful day. Four pink sheep start from underfoot, it seems. They each have one horn dyed bright pink, and their bodies are pinkified. It must be the local dip, or an ID. The road suddenly ends, snapped off by erosion, but I step down onto big heads of marsh grass separated by swampy mud. I don't know what these grasses are called[2], but they seem to me able to sustain my weight as I determinedly press on to circumambulate the Spelga Dam, as one did as a boy in Africa, wary of snakes there but not here, I assume. Perhaps there is a republican moccasin or provo adder secreted in the tassock headed lumps. But they say St Patrick banished all the snakes from Ireland. Things are getting mushier but there's relief ahead. There's a raised

[2] from the agriculture department of the government of Northern Ireland:
Characteristic plant species include devil's-bit scabious, meadow thistle, glaucous sedge, flea sedge, lesser butterfly orchid, water-mint, ragged robin, marsh pennywort and wild angelica. A low coverage of scrub or dwarf shrubs may also occur. Purple moor-grass and rush pasture may sometimes be referred to as fen meadow or rush pasture. Fen meadow is usually found on shallow peaty soils and rush pasture is usually found on mineral soils.

berm of a darker green and sure enough, a path on it. The berm breaks for one, and then a second stream, but someone has laid planks down for crossing. I drop down, the planks depress and mush in, but hold.

The dam is at hand. It's a lovely day, but there's no obvious profusion of animal or bird life. This, I conclude is another holdover from drought-stricken Southern Africa, where water is precious and all the animals and birds flock down to the dams to drink. Here, just pink sheep, cars whining along the road halfway up Slieve Donald. Rain clouds hover but are not shedding. Good thing. I have forgotten my umbrella and rain jacket.

A third rivulet divides the berm, about a yard of clear, babbling water, but no planks. How did they get the planks here? They must have come prepared but I don't think this one through very well.

Instead, the could-have-been-fatal mistake. I reckon if I can get purchase between the end of the berm and the bank of the stream at this one particular narrow bit, I can leap and hope the other side will hold me. On the other side it looks like clear walking to the dam's edge and even onwards to the wall itself.

I think fleetingly of what could be ruined if I plunge in. My eighteenth iPod in three years, my cell phone, my glasses, and so on. Oh, nothing will happen. I drop and prepare to leap.

My front leg plunges in, then the other and in an instant, I am in up to my hips and the quagmire is sucking me down. I thrust my feet down but only sink further.

"El Laurens!! Where's Peter O'Toole when you need him. SHIT!"

I twist my trunk rigorously to my right, jamming my elbows into the earth edge of the berm. Cold Panic. Way above me, a car whines by. I see three cyclists whirr by. I push but my leg sinks deeper. I put all my strength and weight onto my elbows and press down. My legs slowly unstick and start up. I hop my elbows further into the berm and shove with all my might, a power thrust motivated by great fear. My legs come further up and I am able to extricate myself. I lay on the firm earth, gasping.

I look to the skies. I imagine the chopper shot from above. Canadian holidayer disappears.

No foul play.

They'll eventually find someone to say, "He seemed a little depressed, to me."

"If you are not back by three, I'll call out the rescue squad." He is grinning when he says it. The same grin he wore rabbiting on about Land Rovers. Could use one now, with winch.

I look down at my shorts, socks and boots. Absolutely gummed thick with rich Irish swamp mud. I laugh. Looking down, it's like a Turner Prize contender. I right myself after a while.

There's a family van stopped at the lay by high above, about the size of a postage stamp.

I imagine their conversation

"That mahn has garn."

"What mahn?"

"There was a mahn, there, walking along that parth."

They look.

"Theer's naw mahn theer, Rory. Naw git in the van and lot's gaw."

"There was a man theer, Dud."

"A shut yer face. Yar alwees seein thangs."

I now need to get back, and get away from this deceptively benign-looking quagmire. I retrace my steps along the berm, but one of the planks has gone under from my earlier crossing. I stand at the berm's end and pause. I look around, slowly 360 degrees. The clouds are getting a bit darker, the wind is picking up, the temperature dropping. I stop. This is the silent moment. The sky. The wind. I live.

I snap out of it. How am I going to get out, surrounded by perilous swamp?

I put my earphones on and Bowie's greatest hits are paused. Play…

Fame indeed… and off I go, gingerly stepping on dry grass above the muck, making my way up to the road.

Occasionally I sink to my heels.

I have to stop three times to settle my nerves. It is quite lovely in an ominous Windermere kind of way. A few ravens or crows potter about, disappointed I hadn't copped it right there.

But Bowie lifts me up. I never really took Bowie seriously. A magnificent poseur for sure, but no Lennon. So why with all my 1,865 songs and eighty four audiobooks do I choose Bowie at a time like this. He gives bounce, to be sure, patting me upwards like little pegasus wings on my ankles.

At one point, on a dry outburst of thick green grass I actually lie down and roll my legs, first the fronts, then the sides then the backs, and it does a great natural cleaning job, wiping great smears of grey mud on the brushy grasses. If I was going back to any sane companion they might think I just got a wee bit muddy. My sister would greet me with something like, "Playing Hippos, were we?"

After that I am in critical need of a Caesar salad. But on my way to the nearest town, the nearest Tesco's, there's a slowdown, flashing lights, and as I creep by a small red car has somehow hurtled through a tiny village t-junction and levelled a lovely little white stone wall, maybe centuries old, just punched a huge crater through it, and its front is completely concertinaed. There's nobody lying on the ground, no sign of survivors or ambulances, just an accident tow truck, and gaping onlookers. Perhaps someone had a seizure or a bad text. Driverless Demon seed.

Around the corner, a side road leads off and up and there are people lining the horizon. It's one of those moments I used to register but would rarely act on. My life is changed. I can act on pretty well whatever the hell I want to now, pursue any hunch, any whim, any whispering. So I turn around and turn into what turns out to be a cemetery. That's a lot of turns.

The cemetery of St Patrick's Church.

The knot of people I'd seen has moved on, a family it seems, finished with their visit.

When I was a documentary producer in a foreign country, I would check out big cemeteries. It tells you quite a bit about the culture of a people.

Typically for the TV program I worked on, I was sent, not to places I knew a lot about, but to places I knew nothing about. Like Ukraine. Once waiting at a bus stop for a rendezvous at dawn in the middle of nowhere, I wandered into an adjoining cemetery. In the Ukraine, they put pictures of the dead on the tombstones. And medals. And uniforms. A chef's jacket, a barber's scissors, a biker's helmet. The faces display centuries of strange deaths. The fog is icy, bone-cracking. Flocks of starving ravens hop about. It is very Denisovich. For some reason it helps me understand why Ukrainians in 1992 were so fearful and pessimistic.

The first thing one notices about St Patrick's Church cemetery is a row of severed tree trunks, interspersed with plain iron benches. The tombstones spread out for two acres in precise straight lines, many of them black marble with crisp gold lettering, unelaborated fonts. In the middle a fifteen foot high Christ, white as alabaster, pinned to his cross, weeping for the lot of them. There seems to me to be a lot of kids, even infants and young folk interred therein. There is one twenty seven year old ‘murdered’. I do a walk through, thinking of nothing in particular, when I hear an accented voice.

“Would you know when cemetery Sunday is?”

I turn to see a big blonde woman.

“You know I’m just visiting from Canada so have no idea.” (I’m adopting an accent of some kind again. Comes naturally. It makes communication easier, believe me.)

“I’m ten days back from there.”

The speaker looks like Maeve Binchy. A woman in her sixties, very broad and slightly slow-moving, walking stick, emanating warmth.

“Oh really?” I say and we walk towards the path exiting past the row of severed tree trunks.

“Yes, yes. My brother lives there.”

“Really?”

“Yes, yes, just outside of Hamilton.”

Hamilton, an industrial city forty minutes west of Toronto.

“I’m from Toronto.”

“Oh you are, are you?”

“Yes.”

We pass a few graves, me slowing for her gait.

“West Hill. It’s a small place. Very nice.”

“Oh.”

“He used to come here, every year, but he’s not well, so I went over there this time.”

“Okay?”

“Yes. He’s got the angina pretty bad. And cancer too.”

“Oh dear.”

"Well, he can't get insurance to travel here. They want five thousand dollars and he told them to shove it. Although he's visiting his son in Calgary as we speak." She pauses to breathe, then, "So what brings you here?"

"Oh, I was just driving by. Thought I'd pop in, have a look."

"What brings you to Ireland?"

"Oh." Here I never know what to say, a story that will attract as little attention as possible. If one just said the word 'inquisitive' that might be too intriguing. Inquisitive on whose coin? So I try an abbreviated truth.

"Well, I've moved to North Yorkshire, and my wife isn't joining me for a while. I'm semi-retired you see." (I'm starting to talk like them now, see.) "Just thought I'd come over. Never been to Northern Ireland. I'm an avid golfer."

I leave out the fact that I've always been fascinated by the deadly struggle within this European Tribe.

She gestures back to the graves behind us.

"My parents are both buried here, and my husband." She seems quite jolly enough about it. She's got a small clutch of yellow flowers in her right hand.

I decide to go for it.

"I know it's probably a sensitive issue, and I shouldn't pry, because I know really nothing about it, but, I remember reading for such a long time about all the Troubles here and yet, I don't see any expression of it anywhere. But there is one grave where it says clearly and plainly that the young man, twenty seven, was murdered. Is that political or just a crime?"

"Was the script in Gaelic?"

"No."

"Was the font old fashioned and curly?"

"No. It was plain and clear."

"Then it was probably just a crime. As for the Troubles. I was in Belfast through most of it and I never saw anything," she says, then, without missing a beat, to a man who has just joined us from another direction, "So, Aidan. Why did they cut down the trees?"

"They were worried the roots would break up the path," he says, pointing along an asphalt walkway.

"Such a pity," she says.

Sotch.

He continues, "They could have dug a hole and poured diesel into the roots. Or copper nails."

I am nonplussed by the copper nails, and he may have picked that up.

"You hammer copper nails in them, all around the trunk."

And I hear myself saying, like a native, with a slight accent, "Well, I'd rather have a broken path than no trees. The dead appreciate the shade of elms."

"Indeed." They are both nodding their heads vigorously in assent.

We are now at the car park. I put out my hand. I am doing and saying things which catch me by surprise all the time here, like I'm not really whoever I was before I came.

I am unmoored, and not really looking to drop anchor anywhere ever again. She holds on to my hand, affectionately.

"Well, it's been a pleasure meeting you. My name's Robin," I say.

"I'm Ann," she replies.

She lingers, looking back at the strong, ordered graveyard with the Mountains of Mourne reaching above it into a clear blue sky.

"You know, my father said to me. Ann, I want to be buried here, with the mountains, the sea, the fresh air. If you don't get that done, I'll haunt you the rest of my life." She laughs, her whole body shaking. I can feel it through our hands. She turns to me with love in her eyes. "I hope you have a lovely time here."

The political situation in Northern Ireland has remained out of sight. Because of my ignorance, I start way behind. There are bits and pieces, fragments I pick up on, here and there.

In Belfast, I spot a memorial on a street wall, five young laughing faces framed in softened circles, for five young men 'Murdered for their Faith'. I am unable to decipher which faith.

On the Falls road, there are Cubanesque murals of heroic women brandishing large machine guns.

On my last morning in my B and B on the coastal road between Newcastle and Kilkeen, I broach the subject with my host, Bryan the Jeep-mad photographer. It turns out he was in the British Army for five years during the Troubles, but oddly, like Ann in the cemetery "was never part of any incidents." (Is this true, or chosen amnesia? I have seen this before with Rhodesians, Americans, anyone who fought, mostly on the wrong side of history. They don't remember anything. They choose not to remember. Either because they had boring tedious campaigns or quite the opposite.) He continues, not looking at me, but staring outside his bay kitchen window to the Irish Sea with that slight fixed smile on his face. "Today, it's very strange. Division is just below the surface between republicans and unionists."

"Is that union with Ireland?"

He gags. "No, no, no. My God." An incredulous guffaw. "Union with Britain!"

Clearly, he's a unionist.

"Even today, villages within minutes of each other are either republican, or unionist. You can tell by the flags and the bridges."

Echoes of Yugoslavia, I think. When Tito died, neighbours suddenly became Croatians and Serbians, killing each other.

I had noticed very faded Irish colours on one bridge. Green, white and orange. Very close by, a brand new paint job on another bridge displays gleaming red, white, and blue, and the Union Jack flies.

His wife is a primary school teacher. She is particularly upset with a Northern Ireland policy that seeks to introduce Gaelic speaking schools. She reminds me both of English-speaking Quebeckers in Canada and the English in South Africa who dreaded the establishment of French and Afrikaans respectively as official languages. In South Africa, English-speakers looked down on Afrikaans.

This is the same tone. This Irish duo looked down on the language of the Irish. And their Southern neighbours.

There's now the discomfort that comes when locals want a visitor to share their point of view, but it isn't happening.

To lighten the silence I ask if they know where I could see a game of Gaelic Football. I had watched it on television in Canada, and it struck me as an excellent sport, combining rugby, football, handball, and uninterrupted running on an expansive field. But even this game is loaded.

"It's played more in Ireland and those who play it here… well, it's a republican game. They are very intense about it. I played rugby union, and cricket," says Bryan.

He is able to tell me where the nearest GAA field is and I happen across it later in the day. Two games are underway. I see some real skill, eighteen year olds darting and surging across a big field with little interruption from the referee.

Three grey haired men lean against a fence, and one

says, "Looks to me like you are looking for something. Can we help?"

I explain my interest in the game.

"Where are you from?"

"Canada."

"Oh, well then," they say, laughing, "you've come to the right place. This is a tournament organised in the memory of one of ours who spent most of his adult life in… Mississauga."

They call over a woman wearing an official-looking tracksuit.

"Marcie. Here's a Canadian."

She shakes my hand rigorously.

"I'm the Secretary," she says. "You're *most* welcome."

Then I am introduced to the President of the club.

A second lady grabs a group photograph with 'the Canadian'.

They give me an official program. The Dermot Moseley Memorial GAA seven-a-side tournament. There's a picture of him. Upright. Serious. In a black suit. Like a transit manager. Proud.

A player, the son of one of the men, strolls up and chats with his dad, barely a word of which I understand. Red-faced, curly haired, slightly broken nose, sweaty.

They invite me for lunch. But I demur.

"Are there professional GAA players?" I ask.

"No, but we pay the coaches on the QT," one says, then leaning in, sotto voce, "I'm sure you've taken money on the QT at some point, haven't you?"

The question takes me by surprise and I'm struck dumb.

"No, I don't think I have," I say, primly, then, "I must go. I have some errands to run in Newcastle." I lie, and bid them farewell. I should have gone, like the cemetery, but I suspect why I didn't. I didn't want them to find out I wasn't Catholic. My roots are English Protestant.

SUNDAY 21ST MAY

A LONG WALK WITH A PUTTER IS A BEAUTIFUL THING

I am on my way to Royal County Down for a round of golf, booked rashly two days before, jumping the thirty-day pre-booking requirement.

It's rated as the number one golf course in the world, as the stately entrance, and manicured practice greens attest.

Everyone I speak to in Northern Ireland about RCD, as they call it, shake their heads, as if I am about to wrestle the Giant Octopus, recently seen just offshore, in the Irish Sea.

Usually I'm a pretty steady, accurate player, but the wind is up.

After warming up, I pass a man who wears a green bib, some kind of a marshal, an inviting glint in his eye.

"Are you a member?" I ask.

He is grey-haired, stocky, far from the snobby type.

"Oh yes. Sixteen years." Strong accent.

"How do you score on it?"

"Well, funny you should ask. Four years in a row I shot my age, but I thought I wasn't going to keep that up this year, until last week, when I did it again."

He looks very pleased with himself.

"Well, I have to ask. How old are you?"

"Eighty."

"Christ! That's incredible. And at that age. Besides you don't look a day over sixty nine."

He giggles, shaking with good-natured smugness.

"You are a very talented man. And a very lucky golfer to belong here. So... Do you have a tip for me?"

He looks up at the wind in the trees, and winces.

"Such a pity it isn't a fine day for you. Relax. Don't score. You'll never forget this course."

Relax. The second time someone had said that. I wonder if they say that to Death Row inmates?

On the practice putting green, a young man canters up to me and introduces himself as my caddie.

"What's your name?" I ask.

"Andrew," he answers.

"What's your favourite thing outside your job?"

"My dog," he says, chuckling.

We are going to get on just fine.

"Wind's up a bit today. But you just relax."

That word again.

On the first tee, I am introduced to my three playing companions. A threesome from "the Bay area", San Francisco.

My spirits sink a bit. I have to admit Americans are not my favourite golf companions. At these kinds of courses they tend to be humourless, big-headed Republicans, giving themselves all kinds of mulligans, and second chances. Not remotely interested in Canadians.

I can tell from their equipment and attire and demeanour that they are loaded. Not surprising. Clubs should pay Golf Digest for anointing them the number one golf course in the world. That boosts their fees and swells the number of people who come from all over the world to say they have played it. The fee for a round here, two hundred and twenty pounds is twice as much as the average annual income of the West African cocoa farmer.

They invite me to tee off first. Or rather the tall Trump-ish one points imperiously to the tee. "You. Go."

It's a par five with the wind behind us. Massive banks left and dunes right frame a fairway which narrows the more one looks at it.

Relax.

Whack!

I clock my drive straight and true. They nod approvingly as I mumble, "That'll be my best," and check myself for being so negative. Negativity will be my problem all day. The expectation of failure is like a little nuisance dog that doesn't stop barking.

"Good shot. Bark Bark. But what about the next one? Bark. Bark."

I suspect it's because I have already decided the course is going to beat me up. It's like my old high school biology teacher said, "We all think we are better than we actually are." He was unfortunately very ugly, with a face like an orangutan. All wrinkles and a massive pug mouth and nose. But he had the most beautiful wife, seven children and came across as incredibly virile.

He bowled me out once at cricket and would thenceforth greet me with (he had a lisp), "Benger, you're my wabbit." By year three, he'd just say "Wabbit" every time he saw me.

By then he had nine children. His enthusiasm was rapacious.

Two of the Americans pull their drives into the looming bank on the left and re-tee, giving themselves mulligans. The third American has a fused neck disc and only plays from short of the green.

Annoyingly, I don't approve of mulligans. It's like missing with a cruise missile from an aircraft carrier and just getting free shot after free shot until the target is obliterated or the ball finds the middle of the fairway.

"Hell, I hit a good drive on number one." (Ignore the first three attempts.)

I also don't approve of placing the ball. Or giving any putts. Play it as it lays. A bit of a puritanical prick on the links, I am.

My ball is nestled on the perfectly cut fairway. It is like the baize of a snooker table. Instead of revelling in it, the perfection of it all unnerves me.

On the second tee, I'm feeling unrelaxed and almost

miss my drive completely, duck hooking the ball into the fescue forty yards ahead.

The wind is starting to sound like a siren no one can turn off.

On the third, at the top of my swing, I see that I have teed the ball very low and sure enough launch a line drive straight into the top of a cliff guarding the fairway ahead. Despite going straight to the exact wisp of grass it hit, it too is a goner, unfindable, buried deep within.

Three holes, two lost balls.

On the fourth, a famous par three over solid gorse and gaping trench bunkers, we turn bang slap into the wind.

"How strong is this wind?" I ask Andrew, who has been busy telling me about his beloved Aikido dog, showing me a picture of a mutt with an Irish green choker.

"Thirty mile an hour, gusting to forty."

The tee is elevated, the pin 180 yards away.

Andrew hands me my three wood, which I hit 200 yards. But the wind feels like a wall and I lose my balance on my practice swing. Then it knocks my ball off the tee. The Americans are tickled.

I am just about to throw my club at the ball when Andrew steps in, just like the pros. He hands me my driver, which I usually hit about 250.

"The other fellas say you should use this."

I stand over the ball.

When it's breezy, swing easy. Relax.

I hit it perfectly. The ball flies all the trouble, the wind stops it dead above the green, and it drops pin high, 25 feet left.

"Happy days," says Andrew, handing me my putter on the tee. "A long walk with a putter is one of the most beautiful things in golf, now."

I par the hole.

We climb to another elevated tee.

Andrew is back to his dog.

"When I get home after a long day at the course, my little aikido is there, and he just goes crazy. My girl and I love him so much we've decided not to have any children."

He's babbling on, but I find it quite pleasant.

Then I noticed a large slinky black thing dart from one bush to another just beyond the teebox. He spots it too.

"What's that?"

"A cat. Probably wild."

"Feral."

"Yes. May have started out domestic but they live off mice and baby rabbits out here."

"I don't particularly like the idea of a black cat crossing my path right now."

"Ah, superstitious are you. Yes. Well. Here in Ireland..."

(I wonder if this is code for republican.)

"...we have a superstition about magpies," he says. "See one, it's bad luck. See two, good luck. See three, you're getting sex. See four, you're in the money."

Black cat or no, the next five holes are also into the teeth of the gale. It's really just a strong wind, but golfers are like fishermen, and for the purposes of this report, it's a gale. And it kills me. A double and four triples. I'm hitting my approaches okay but they stop in mid-air and boomerang wildly off-target. And putting on the saucer greens is simply beyond me. By the ninth I am undone. Little Irish banshee wind gremlins have bored into my brain and are singing 'Danny Boy' at chipmunk speed. I stand over the ball as if I have never played the game before. My arm muscles are trembling with the indignation of being attached to my trunk. So I start behaving poorly.

When the grinning Californians assemble for the customary group shot with the Mountains of Mourne and the windswept bay and all the beauty of this majestic track in the background, I scuttle off like a pickpocket.

First nine, 54. I contemplate throwing in the towel.

Andrew the caddy is undeterred. "You know, Robin, I like your style. You just drop another ball and get on with it. Some of these other guys get so upset."

Clearly he misses the tempest within.

On the tenth tee, one of the caddies offers me a smoke and I grab it. Before my companions return from the halfway house, I mis-hit my hybrid six from 200 yards, but a three club wind carries it almost into the hole. A caddy calls out, "Make mine a Macallan," as it trickles up towards the pin. "Mine a double," says the other as it kisses the flag and stops above the hole.

"I topped it," I say.

Andrew says, "Happy days. No pictures on the scorecard."

He hands me my putter. And again, "In golf, a long walk with a putter is a beautiful thing."

It is six feet above the hole, six feet for birdie. I three putt, like a drunk.

After that, I play very well. On the par five twelfth, I draw a long drive towards a humongous bunker. My caddie thinks it kicks left into the fescue but one of the other caddies spots it in good position on the fringe of the fairway.

"Happy days," says Andrew.

I put a five iron onto the green.

He hands me my putter and is about to say it again when I ask him about the Troubles.

"All before my time. But if somebody asks me my last name, I don't tell them because I know they want to know my fecking religion. Once they know that, they think they know everything. I say my prayers every night, for sure, but I don't go to church anymore."

The Americans are strangely vacant, devoid of interesting conversation, speaking only in golf clichés.

"Can you believe that?" "That's not fair." "Macho man!"

There's something bloodless about them. They are like Robots of the Trump Imperium. Now I'm conflating, I am. I get on better with the caddies, and bum two more cigarettes because they seem to be helping my ball striking, which is more important at this moment than my health.

On the eighteenth par five, back into the wind, I need a par to break a hundred, and the fairway beckons, shining golden-white in the late sunlight. It is one magnificent sight after another, centerfolds of golf gorgeousness, a bit otherworldly. Thinking eagle, I pull my drive spectacularly onto the next fairway. From there, going against the conservative advice of my caddy ("play out"), I try to hammer my three-wood over a copse, but it's no Dunsinane, and ball #5 is lost. I take an illegal drop and pull my five wood. Smash. Gone. #6. Another illegal drop and I blast out of the fescue to five feet for a dubious eight.

48 for the nine for a 102.

I am dissatisfied that my game hasn't held together. I pay Andrew the fifty pounds caddie fee, but he wants a tip. I tell him I already am over-budget (two hundred and seventy pounds for the day) and mention that documentary filmmakers don't have as much money as rich Americans. His disappointment is ameliorated slightly when I follow his orders and drop his pocket tag into the EXCELLENT slot in the pro shop, rather than the SATISFACTORY or UNSATISFACTORY one.

I get into the car and for an hour drive like James Hunt on crack. By the time I reach the village in County Wicklow several hours later, where I am staying, I am unwound.

The next day, Monday the 22nd, I meander back towards Dublin for the night ferry to Liverpool.

Along the way, I stop randomly whenever I see the

wee brown Golf Course sign with the little cream flag. And there are a lot of them. Most of them hidden gems. Woodenbridge, Wicklow, Bray. Between ten and thirty pounds a round. In forest and vale and above the coast.

I resolve to stick to hidden gems from now on. I will never master the great courses. My days of slaying dragons are over, especially at that price.

Tomorrow I am booked on the Magical Mystery Bus Tour on the fiftieth anniversary of Sergeant Pepper's Lonely Hearts Club band, and Wednesday I am at Headingley for the SA v England cricket match.

MONDAY/TUESDAY 22ND/23RD MAY

DUBLIN WRITERS AND THE MANCHESTER BOMBING

The highlight of my three hours in Dublin is the cafe above Books Upstairs, where I write and read among other readers and writers. To be anonymous among a foreign gathering of readers and writers is warming. In a way, these are my people, a home abroad. Go to the harbour, or the riverside, and find where the writers read and sip coffee. And be healed, or fortified. I get details on the Dublin International Book Festival. Just a fantastic line-up but all in the evenings, starting at eight, and I have to be on my ferry at seven thirty pm.

The ferry from Dublin is a real tub. My red Vauxhall is dwarfed by heavy rigs. There about fifty truckers in the cafeteria. It's not just a cliché. Truckers are big, display tattoos.

My cabin is rudimentary, definitely a trucker's cot. We pull out at nine thirty pm. I stand on the outside deck, facing astern, leaning on the rails, watching the sun go down behind Dublin, watching the wake. I've been so blessed to see so many of the world's great waterways, and it's deeply soothing, and meditative. The Great Oceans and Rivers. And often, I hear Otis Redding's voice as I sit in the evening sun. I'm smoking a cigarette, looking at the little LS Lowry stick people taking an evening walk along a long jetty south of the harbour entrance, a very good walk, noted for next time.

In my cot. There's just enough room on a small table to set up my laptop and write, the porthole at eye level offering the sight of the Irish sea, and islands and the coast north of Dublin as night falls. The soft languorous slow fades to night that happen here at this time of year. I write for an hour or so, then head back to the cafeteria with my Rooibos teabag for hot water. A couple with a baby, the only other non-truckers I see, and a couple of the truckers slump in a lounge watching something that is out of my sightline. I pop my head around the corner, sure enough, it's TV. I don't quite register Manchester Breaking News, until I see the ambulances' blue flashing lights and the next crawl line. Suspected explosion.

One's heart just sinks now. Ever since the Sri Lanka cricket team was strafed by a jihadist group in Pakistan, I have thought it inevitable that suicide bombers would target mass secular events like sports matches, rallies and concerts. There's a 'here-we-go-again', sinking feeling to these events, and one wonders how free, instant global publicity is part of the suicide bombers' thinking. Screens as far away as Beijing and Sydney, right around the electrified world, are lighting up with the news of the Manchester arena bombing. I've never heard of Ariana Grande. This one is so mean, though. Teenage girls. Is the killer targeting this crowd because of the affront she represents to his version of Islam, and the 'proper' place for females? This question is never dealt with in what I see of the saturation coverage in the coming days. It's just so low.

Whether it is that, the fact that we are docking at five, or the five cappuccinos I'd had during the day, or the grumbling of the big screws juddering through the thin walls of my compartment, I can't sleep. The public address orders us to our vehicles at five thirty am but one of the rigs, backing down, strikes the side of the ramp. It takes workmen an hour to fix it. So I sit in the car listening to the live reports, the panic, the nuts and bolts embedded, the Manchester horror show.

I can barely think of an act more cowardly, but of course, the mainstream reaction is predictable and nobody, for the two days I listen on the radio, nobody talks about what Corbyn had raised in the election campaign. That the War on Terror isn't working. You have to address poverty in the Islamic world, and marginalise the maniacal strains of Islam best you can. Since 9/11, what is working? In Trump we have the worst actor in the most powerful seat. The man cannot wait to shed some serious blood, which will just breed more blood.

At eleven thirty, I've booked on the Magic Mystery Beatles fiftieth anniversary of Sergeant Pepper's Lonely Hearts Club Band Bus Tour*, the longest appellation for a bit of tourist frippery, for sure. I have two hours to kill, so I just walk, along the Mersey, east, inland. The old communities have been erased or adapted for million dollar flats, riverside condos and offices. The walkway is pristine stone. Only the old original bollards remain, thick bulbous-headed black reminders of the hawser-stretching days of docking and loading, shipping in and shipping out.

Outside the Liverpool Exhibition Hall and the big concert venue at Albert Dock, men in dark blue overalls are lowering the flags to half-mast. A man who looks Filipino is trying to get a jammed Union Jack to descend, but it's not co-operating. He slams the hollow metal flag post with impatience. Still it doesn't budge.

The river is brown-sluggish. There's a Sterling Hayden-faced old codger with three rods in the water.

"What are you catching here?" I ask.

"Nothing right now," he says, in the thick Scouser accent.

"What can you get out of here?"

"Well, somebody pulled a skate out yesterday."

"How heavy?"

"Seven pounds."

"Woo. That would keep you going for a while."

He rhymes off three other kinds of fish he's caught, bass is one.

It's not an interesting walk, past car dealerships, those Range Rovers again and the Jaguar outlet. The designs of new Jaguar are so modular and homogenous, the old teardrop grille and swooped lines long gone. Man's ability to homogenise a successful design in the name of mass marketing. Profits equal meddling equals mediocrity. I read in the financial press that Jag sales are spiking thanks to increased demand for luxury cars from the Middle East and Africa. Corruption and Greed and Instant Status.

At ten, I go to the MMT50AOTROTSPLHB* office, but I've booked for the next day by mistake and both today's bus trips are full. However they get me on the eleven o'clock. The guide went to Lennon's schools and the driver played with Pete Best. The guide, Jay Johnson, is a bit brusque but he's authentic and a good storyteller. But the quality of the music he plays is muddy. It turns out that John and Paul were middle-class lads, though the guide didn't point out that John was staying in Aunt Mimi's Mendips because dad had split for the open seas and his mum couldn't afford lodging for them. We sit in the bus outside the Yoko-owned house as Johnson points out where Julia, his mum, is struck and killed by a drunken off duty policeman.

After the tour, I thank Jay but gently point out that the music is muddy.

This pisses him off.

"Well, mate, it's a bluddy bus. You are not going to get bluddy Bose speakers on bluddy bus," waving me off brusquely.

I go and have a salad at Gregg's and brood about this. It's The Beatles. It's about the music. Part of my motive energy always comes from an irresistible desire to complain when things aren't right. But nobody else ever does. It is true during the apartheid years. A miniscule number of whites complain. Miniscule. It's not apartheid but… I walk back down to the office and complain.

"New high quality music would enhance your product," I say, taking the business argument, rather than the musical one.

The three men on duty, or two should I say, as the third has his head locked into his cell phone during the whole discussion. The two men have no idea what I am talking about. They are just grunts earning a few quid at the low end of a Beatles industry that brings in eighty five million pounds a year to the Liverpool economy. Real Nowhere Men locked in eight days a week.

As I drive to Leeds, the misery of Manchester just keeps pouring out of the radio. The loss of children is a life sentence.

My B and B in Headingley is run by a rather dolorous hippie who tells me twice the same story of a tenant who ripped her off. I find a local restaurant and have 'bang bang' chicken salad, and crash at nine thirty, exhausted.

WEDNESDAY 24TH MAY

PLAYING LIKE GOD

The cricket match starts on Wednesday at two, so to kill two birds with one stone I google golf and find the nearest course. It's five minutes away, and as far away from Royal County Down as one can imagine.

It's a community course on what must have been a country estate in the age of the Brontes. It was built in 1812 for the mother-in-law of a prominent Leeds businessman, designed by Sir Robert Smirke who designed the British Museum. In the 1920s it falls into disrepair, is taken over by a charity, with the proviso that its wide green spaces were to be dedicated to the leisure of the people. Opposite of the exclusivity of much private property in England. Gott's Park Public Golf Course emerged and today eighteen holes cost nine quid. The first five holes are extremely hilly, cardiac. The heat is stifling. At thirty degrees, it's the hottest day of the year. In England. In May!!

The course is overgrown, the tees rough, the greens as

slow as an unmown lawn. I love it. There're dog walkers all over the place. I get my exercise, play shitty golf, but no mind. At one point there are four back-to-back zig-zag par threes, unique in my experience. One of the most bizarre courses I have played. And not *one other* player. I'm done by twelve noon. There is no real pro shop, just a girl who takes green fees and sells tees and candy bars.

The cricket match starts with the expected memorial minute of silence to the victims of Manchester. I want to reach out to the players of South Africa, to tell them how well I know them, what they represent to me. The South African cricket team with its six players of colour is for me personally, the public flowering of a principled private stand I took forty six years ago fighting racism in sports, when it was unpopular and drew a hostile crackdown. The team has Moslem and Hindus from Durban, coloureds from the Cape, blacks from Johannesburg, Afrikaners from Pretoria, English guys from the Eastern Cape and the mining towns of the Highveld.

The crowd, the event is heavenly. These are my people, this is my sporting culture even though I support the opposition. I watch raptly like a man taken to the oasis of something after more than forty years in the desert. I love cricket so much. I follow every ball, intently. The English team plays very, very well. It is unrecognisably bold compared to the coma-inducing elevens of the '60s and '70s. Hard-bitten grinders like Boycott, Barrington and Edrich, who would bat for three days at a glacial pace.

Thank God they've been replaced by the Flintoffs, Stokes and Bairstows of recent years.

At one point my phone rings. It is the ticket office at the ground. A steward has handed in two passports with my name on them. They must have fallen out of my back pocket, though God knows when and where. Very odd. I collect them with relief and over-the-top gratitude.

South Africa plays uncharacteristically poorly. England trounces them.

After the match I drive home to Castle Howard. The hour it takes floats by thanks to an excellent BBC radio documentary about the making of Sergeant Pepper's. It seems Lennon is insatiable, coming in every day with a new idea which George Martin would often provide the sound for. A choir. A horn. They work long, hard hours. LSD obviously plays its part in igniting Lennon's perception of ordinary everyday things. A newspaper article, a street sign, gates from his girl-chasing youth. (A Day In The Life; Penny Lane; Strawberry Fields Forever.)

SATURDAY/SUNDAY 27/28TH MAY

THE WOUNDED DRUM AND THE FACE PAINTER

So it was a day or two
of walking round Ampleforth
and golf and cricket
and walking round Malton
and the face painter at the food show.

The thing about living here
is this
If the day dawns
blank and empty
One looks for a walk
and sallies forth.

On the way to walk near Ampleforth
I find the golf course
we couldn't in the dark.

It’s a hut in a wood
a self serve place
18 holes
for eleven pounds
into the yellow wooden honour box.
Quite thrilling
and I shall play it Monday

On the walk,
from the Jane Eyre audiobook
I hear a speech
about isolation
a speech laid hard upon the head of one
that *she’s* come from who knows where
to seek something from *us*
only for *herself*,
but will always be an outsider
and must not be admitted into our circle
but I cannot
find it
now.
It is about me,
the too many places
that I am from
to pin me down
and thus to know
exactly who should be admitted
where it’s a possibility
which it isn’t.

Saturday there is the weekly Clutch at Scarborough South
Two quid in the kitty
betterball four ball
against the field,
my partners, Frank who slams it straight
a lean and callow cricketer called John
who walks very fast

And Jim
a Scot
"from the lowlands between
Edinburgh and Glasgow"
who hits it straight too
and swears a blue Scottish treat
over his short game
"What the fuck d'ya think ya doooin'
ya fuckin' eediot,"

and when he sees me win three holes
he starts to say
"C'man Rrrrobin" after each tee shot
with the cascading rolling RRR
cheering me on
with fierce hope.
Eyes squinting against rain
And disappointment.

Frank birdies two in a row, and
we blow that lead and lose 2 down
and off I go in pursuit of Slingsby 2nd X1
in Huby 35 minutes away
down Robin's Lane
past the pub called
The Wounded Drum.

Tucked away
(where else)
a ramshackle pavilion and scoreboard
Vince the captain with whom I'd spoke
is compiling a stylish left handed 38

An aged couple with an ancient black and white terrier
as fat as a piglet
look
like the retired Club President
and his widowed sister
While
a handsome Asian physician
asks a Pakistani radiologist
about his residency
and stumbling out from the changing room
with long white hair hanging down
beneath a floppy hat,
a man who looks like
the well retired bass player
for Pink Floyd

waits his turn to bat
and gets it
Only to run himself out
Declaring loudly at tea
to Vince the captain
"I cannot run"
as if he, the skipper, were to blame
but what is he to do?
"It's stressful every Saturday,"
says Vince
when finally
we speak
"To put a team together"
but didn't ask me if I played.
How old do I look?
Does he know I once drove Procter for four.
Only Umpiring, I say, wanting the offer.

He later sent me scads and scads of rules and regulations
about the senior cricket league
and I fathom that
he doesn't want to
be blamed for an umpire
who doesn't know what he's doing.

And then
today
a Malton walk
past yet another cricket pitch

where nine year olds
Old Malton Boys team
Is bowling
Driffields out for 30-odd.

and Yes
I thought
I'd have preferred my boys did this
in their whites
on the green
rather than
ice hockey and rib-cracking hits
padded, swishing by, faces covered,
stitches in their gums
in cold, dark, grunting TO.

I did what I could
discharging paternity
though my heart
was only partly in it
the one sport I dislike.

And now a church
St Mary The Virgin
from the 11-hundreds
surrounded by ancient tombstones
that still say
'much loved'
'died in hope'

'beloved'
everyone dies with the same hope
in religion.

Inside a lady with severe shoes
offers a tour and free water
I decline
she says
"Then rest, rest. Be calm"
pointing to a pew
so I do, sip
and look about
a church founded by a crippled saint
who insisted on women (nuns)
being accepted and built 9 other churches
and several orphanages
was canonised
in 1202
by
Pope Innocent 111
St Gilbert of Sempringham.

As he passes me on the aisle
The curate asks
"How long have you been going?"
"About an hour,
I parked on the other side of the river, in Norton."
"Ahaa" and on he passes.

The walk continues out of town down a dusty
Transvaal road
to Eden Camp
a former German and Italian POW site
where the original huts have been turned into a world
war two museum
one, for example
a U boat
very dark and stifling inside,
with ocean burblings,
depth charge and torpedo sound effects.

Another, Hitler's Rise
has a remarkable photograph
which explains fanaticism
how people like him
and Amin and Stalin
come to power
Its writ clear
On the faces of young men and girls staring,
Drinking him in
as if he is The Saviour

In other huts, the blitz
how people slept
in tunnels
and corrugated iron garden sheds
children evacuated
All quite

Moving
thoughts of my own parents
Dad with the 8th in Africa
and Italy
Mum nursing wounded victims
It's in the blood somewhere,
anxious, sad
And impotent

Then the food fair in Malton
the whole town shut down
stall after stall after stall
of Henderson's Relish, Fudge, Yorkshire Wine, pulled pork BBQ burgers, cheese,
drummers, ales, wild hawks, china, goldfish, and the face painter from Hull.
I want a shandy and a savoury thing,
and won't be stopped
or diverted
All the bartenders under the tent
have spectacular Bowie-like sparkle-fans under their eyes.
I ask for a shandy
"We're out of lemonade."
I leave the bar and find a store with lemonade
"will that be all, sir?"
"yes"
"one pound"
"there"
"thank you"

back to the bar
“A Blonde Lady please”
“Pint or Half?”
“Half please”
“in a pint plastic container?”
got it
tried to leave to fetch paid for pulled pork burger
but security stops me
“can’t leave with beer sir”
so no place to leave beer
except
The face painter’s table
whose face
and arms
are extravagantly painted
“yes of course”
she says
Get burger, return
add lemonade
nowhere to sit
nice face painter
“Sit here, sir”
place beer and burger there
‘Where are you from?”
“‘‘Ull”
“Where?”
“Ull”
“O Hull”
“Where ya from?”

she is beautiful
with strange orange red hair
"Canada"
and then it is over
and I come home
on bank holiday Sunday
to do me laundry
in trailer park.

MONDAY 29TH MAY
THE COMPLEXITIES OF LAUNDRY

Laundry is about the most complicated thing I do nowadays. I need two dollars worth of twenty pence coins for the dryer. I head into Malton, to Morrisons, do twenty pounds worth of shopping and the cashier is delighted to give me eight twenty pence coins. I need two old pound coins for the washer. That's for two hours. The dryer may or may not take sixty minutes. The controls on the machines are devilishly complicated. One mistake and it can prolong the business. And the dryer never seems to quite dry everything. It takes a whole half day.

A gypsy or traveller family has taken up residence on the bank of the road between the caravan park and Malton. Their three small ponies are tethered close by, cropping the grass between the road and the property line of a farm. A sign offers knife sharpening.

I watch the first half of the third ODI between England

and South Africa. Rabada bowls brilliantly, Parnell very well. Amla, who dropped a sitter in the previous match takes two beauties at first, as does Faff at second. England is 20 for 5.

At lunchtime, I go to Ampleforth for golf. It's a very hilly nine hole in fine condition, and I have it to myself. I can't par anything. At the top of the hill, two cricket fields appear. It's the Yorkshire girls Under-17 tournament, four teams from each quadrant of the county. The standard of play seems very good, and there is much enthusiasm. An overcast day.

TUESDAY 30TH MAY

CRACKED JOHN AND THE COAL MINE

Reflecting on the day that's past
First: sad news of my mate John P;
then down a mine
great history and a profound end.

first Johnny P
the onetime crackerjack political fixer
fell on his face
into the shite

his mind cracked up at 62
alzheimer's froze his crackling brain
all the balls in the air
Wives and children,
Several Mayors
A Premier
PMOs
private lines and complex schemes

lobbyists and unions
oiling the machine
and those with dough
all came crumbling down
It turns out
to his wife's alarm
Johnny's had a secret second life
another wife
and daughter too
using her money
to pay for them too

His Big Rich Life
blows up overnight
into a thousand shards
cutting him off
kicking him out
save a circle of comrades
who answer the call

I because he is a Canadian who
understood that apartheid had to be
brought down
crashing
treated like a cancer
he united all the anti apartheid factions
I saw him do it and want him to know
the people of South Africa say thank you
even though he never received a damn thing

not a dollar or rand
not the Order of the Baobab
Only a handshake from Mandela.

As a journo
I'd covered him winning
both city and province
and almost
with his boyhood buddy Layton
the whole damn country
devoted to a fault
fighting for us
until he fucked up
and under the bus
they threw poor John
as hard as a brick
as bold as the first man over the trench
and into the fray
I once saw him punch a man
who'd stolen his son's golf ball.

So for many months
I've taken him out
shuddering with shame
racked with sobs
searching for the name
of his own three kids
or is it four? Or five.
Couldn't keep his fly shut.

We walk
down by the river
through the woods
stopping for birdsong
it always seems
the longer he is out
the more he comes back
the more comes back

and now this from his caretaker
just to let us know
the turn he's taken
"John isn't aware of the approximate time of day, the weather, and what season or year we are in. His memory is worsening and many times he is unable to complete sentences or thoughts. On several occasions he dresses for a very cold day when it's really warm outside."

He's going going
dear John
I miss him
Here I bet
I could bring him alive
in the Yorkshire vales
there in a city that's turned its back
on all he's done
wifeless
childless
he can't remember

what all went wrong.
He is getting stomped incomprehensibly
Through the ground.

Thinking of John
puts my own extremely good fortune
Into relief
as I drive south towards the Museum of Coal Mining.

About three this morning I wake from a dream
I don't know what it is about but
I've been dreaming rich here of late
and it leaves me thinking of going down a mine today.

I have two coal mining stories.
One.
I am in Donetsk,
The Coal Basket of the Soviet Union
Ukraine
in February '03
before the current crisis
and we, a documentary crew, were supposed to go down
a coal mine
but when I saw the clattery condition of the antiquated wooden lift and the deep black on the faces of the Ukrainian coal miners coming up
I said no
we will see nothing
and coal dust will wreck the equipment

we will get the pictures we need
to illustrate the importance of the coal region to Russia
and Ukraine
through surface pictures
and we got them in the wash house
the men stripped to their waists
chain-smoking
black faced
broken-nosed
Life Expectancy 47
Rampant respiratory diseases
the soundman whispers in my ear
"No wonder they stopped Hitler"

The other is the description of Paul Morel's dad
in DH Lawrence's Sons and Lovers
the grime of it
the pit of it
the coming home drunk and black-raged
fury of it.

Of course there was reading about
Scargill v Thatcher
and it looking like a battle to the death of something
a class war
the end of the coal industry in Britain.

One of my audiobooks
YORKSHIRE: GOD'S OWN COUNTRY

by Gary McKracken
he talks about the coal museum
a "moosan't miss"
but more importantly he talks about
the death of the industry
with heartfelt anger,
soul and culture smothered and forever gone
"it makes ma blood boil"

So off I go
down the pit
for a few quid
with about three families
guided by
Kevin
a third generation miner
61 years in the mine
including the touring thing
started at fifteen
in 1956
200 feet below
he shows us a woman on all fours
a hauler in a 3 foot hole
strapped around the waist
"that would be me ma"'
and he sitting in the dust-hot dark for 12 hours
opening and closing a door
switch off yer lamps
and so we did

inky
doesn't do it justice
"In that"
the old miner said
"12 hours, 5 days a week,"

and turning in a practised move
his light upon a life size pony
"and they *lived* down here."

"The comradeship."
he shakes his head
"The comradeship
was fantastic down here.
It'd kill me now
but I would do it again
if I could"

"In 1913 there were 1 million miners in Yorkshire field, life expectancy 45. There's still 200 years worth of coal here"
hitting the black gleaming seam with his gloved hand
"but we were killed by politics"
"and environment" I said
which he ignores
no talk
of Green
down 'ere

It is a world down there
unimaginable
with the gas
and the flooding
and the noise
and the fact that
you paid for the equipment
and if it broke
so were you.

Unimaginable dark
underground world
all the owners joined the mines together
a rabbit warren of creaking groaning dripping
passageways deep beneath the earth

I thought if the Nazis had occupied Britain
the resistance could have hid and lived down here
But the Germans would have pumped
Poison Gas down the shafts
a tomb for a nation
whose non-members
and subservients
would shed not a tear.

Britain is subsiding
and something stirs to replace Her.

It is a moving, must-see mine tour, which I love and I love Kevin the guide.

I ask him at one point how many fatalities back in the day and am surprised at how few. One every seven months. Safer than the buses, he says. I remember the incredible safety record at INCO where I had worked in a smelter for one winter, 1972/3, in Sudbury.

"Yes I know, I worked in a mine," I blurt out. Because I want to be close to him? It isn't exactly true. I worked in the smelter of a mine, above ground. It's like saying you were in the war, but actually operating a radio in a warm office somewhere safe, inland, protected from the blasts and the bullets.

"Where?" he perks up.

"Canada."

"This is from Canada." He pats a huge mechanical driller.

And thenceforth Canada references are plentiful.

On the surface, he tells two other ex miners, "He's a miner from Canada!"

"Well, not exactly. I worked three months in the fluid bed roaster at the Copper Cliff nickel smelter in Sudbury."

"Ooh nickel," they say. "Nice and clean."

I buy a bacon and chicken sandwich at the Mine Museum café, then go out on their nature trail for a long walk.

I listen to Frederick Forsyth's autobiography 'The Outsider' most of the way. He is down to his last sou, fired from every Fleet Street newspaper and the BBC for going against the grain in his coverage of the Biafran War.

He thrashes out his mega-selling Day of the Jackal in thirty five days. It's rejected by every publisher because "no reader would believe in the assassination of a President who is alive", but it's picked up by a man he meets at a party, a publishing executive, who buys the rights for five hundred pounds.

I am walking along the road an hour away from the mining museum and see the magical sign, public footpath. I cross a field. Coming in the other direction, a young blonde girl in farming overalls is walking a manic brown and white spaniel who's describing huge circles on a training leash, devouring scents, in ecstasy. The path narrows through nettles and I cover my legs before dropping alongside an ancient wood. The path drops to reveal an ugly red brick village.

In my ears, Frederick Forsyth has made it to an airport during the terrible Nigerian kwashiorkor epidemic, but there are no flights out. I have been there too, in my memory. Mozambique. Somalia. To witness death in these places is to rip a layer out of your soul forever. And the hundreds of others, desperate to get out to save their lives, yet you, the white journalist, will have priority.

The path bends between two houses and reveals… yet another cricket field. They seem to spring up wherever I go in Yorkshire, this one really unmown. A ramshackle sign reads Flockton Cricket Club. I reach a bench on the high side beneath the trees, looking over the grass pitch to the spire-spiked horizon beyond, the western edge of Leeds.

In my ears, Forsyth spots Irish nuns piling on to a decrepit DC-4 with dying babies. It's a rescue flight by the owner of the crate, a South African called van der Merwe. He accepts Forsyth's offer to be co-pilot.

They take off in complete darkness. Over the delta, one of the two port engines gives out. Forsyth looks back into the plane. Babies, nuns amidst the stench of vomit and diarrhoea. Then the starboard outer engine begins to die. Van der Merwe begins to sing Afrikaans hymns. Forsyth stares out of the window at the moon and the approaching ocean waters. I see it. I have been there, in rickety planes clattering out of famine zones. On the horizon they see the lights of land. Finally the wheels clear the sand dunes as the engine cuts out and they bang down onto the Libreville runway. Red Cross ambulances spirit the children away.

Forsyth and van der Merwe linger in the cockpit, that moment when you realise how close it's been. Van Der Merwe prays. Forsyth listens to the ticking of the engine blocks in the night. I, too, have listened with huge relief to the ticking of the engine blocks in the night.

I rip the earphones off, and drink in the cricket-quiet birdsong and tree-wind rustle around me.

I imagine miners play their cricket here. For decades. Respite in the sunshine, their wives in their summer dresses in the breeze that sweeps up the valley, in the air, above the darkness and the pits below.

I am eating my lunch on a bench they might have sat on

too. There's something marvellous about it all, a miracle really, life, here, history, deep battles, tomorrow.

It's an hour back. John will have forgotten me by now. Forever. Not the way he would have wanted it.

Corbyn is closing fast. I like him from the get-go much to the scepticism of my Labourite friends here, who when I arrived feel he is a disaster and leading them to extinction. May is way, way ahead when she calls this election. But Corbyn is thoughtful, understandable, ordinary in the best way, and cleverer than they think. In comparison, May is the captain of the Titanic and she's just spotted the iceberg. I think Corbyn may do a Trudeau. Overtake the incumbent in the final furlong, and, dare I say, win it going away. My friends shake their heads.

WEDNESDAY 31ST MAY

THE FALL OF A TIGER

I'm always sad to see May end. Living in the northern hemisphere, it's become my favourite month, as it's the one furthest away from winter.

Driving to golf this morning, the green of the North Yorkshire fields and woods are eye-aching.

I have a day of rejections.

I stop in Malton for a coffee and get stuck in the queue. Then two knots of traffic. I am ten minutes late for the Clutch sign up at Scarborough and although there are tee-off times available, the one guy I speak to seems to think nothing can be done.

"We're all full up. No chance."

Back in Canada they would split a foursome if a single golfer arrived late but not these geezers, set in their ways. I wonder if the overseas membership (half what they are paying) makes me a second class member.

I pop into the pro shop to see if I can salvage my round. After eleven years the pro, Tony has been fired, as I understand it. There's some kind of a dispute about the money he makes from the pro shop. He seems more passionate about his other job as an Elvis impersonator, and is not interested in giving golf lessons anymore. He'd much rather be Elvis than Ian Poulter. Golf is a peculiar living, an odd culture altogether, and the latest news about Tiger Woods lances a boil at the heart of it.

Tony says I can slot in behind the Clutch foursomes and play alone, which I am very happy to do. I am happiest lost in my own mind and game on a golf course. As I go around, my mind wanders to a form of revenge for this exclusion. I am, in Canada, a 14 handicap, but here I have only broken 90 once, an 89, which makes me a 18-21 handicap. I am going to enter all the scores and present that handicap and start pissing them off by winning, although they are a tough bunch of coots, and will have a riposte. An appeal. Potential for controversy.

As for Tiger Woods. He is found asleep in his vehicle at three am on Monday morning and is clearly out of it. He says he's having a bad reaction to drugs he is taking in the wake of a fourth back operation. His Mercedes, which is still running, is banged up on the driver's side. The police take him in, take a mug shot and release him around ten am.

I think a lot about Tiger on my sole round of golf today. I think about how magnificent he was in his prime. For twelve years he is dominant, furlongs ahead of the rest of the field in a game where the margins of victory, at the top, are slim. He wins fourteen majors. His style is extremely aggressive, added to a magical touch around the greens. There is not a scintilla of self-doubt in his approach. They redesign entire courses to counter his power and length. But he adapts, as he does when he wins one of his Opens using irons. Tiger Woods was unstoppable.

I am one of the thousands of Canadians who watch him play what he describes as his best shot ever. It is on the eighteenth hole at Glen Abbey golf course, the final round of the 2000 Canadian Open. He has a one-stroke lead over playing partner Grant Waite of New Zealand. He pounds an enormous drive right into the bunker short of the water on the right, giving him no perceivable shot, from 216 yards out. Waite, a steady lefty is on in three. The rain starts to come down. Woods lashes a six iron over the lip, over a tree, over the water, and it lands beyond the green, spins back and stops on the fringe.

I'd been following him for five holes and that is the best of three incredible shots hit with tremendous self-confidence and mental strength.

Now he is a wreck.

I've always been fascinated by his blackness in a sport which is the whitest, most conservative sport in the world. Apart from Harold Varner 111, ranked 138th in the world, no American Black follows Tiger's extraordinary breakthrough.

He has behaved impeccably on this subject, never publicly stirring the pot, putting millions into a Foundation which helps inner city kids learn the sport.

His marriage to a very white beauty, like OJ Simpson's, came crashing to a halt when it is revealed that he is a serial philanderer.

On the course, his vicious, torqueing technique is breaking down his body. But there's something else. In his various attempted comebacks, he sprays his drives, suffers from chip-yips and cannot sink those dramatic putts. Mentally he seems shot.

And now this.

It's a tragedy, although the cynics will shed no tears for Tiger. He is worth multiple millions and will stay that way regardless of whether he ever competes in a golf tournament again. I wonder if he has any motivation to do so. They say he spends his life playing videogames and being dad to his two kids.

His alienation from all is clear to see. One fears a tragic end. One fears for the impact of this crash for young black athletes everywhere.

Why bother? Look what they did to Tiger. Look what it did to him.

I am playing in exquisite conditions, quite well, until the last three holes which I double bogey.

I don't know what it means. Other than this.

Man, even given everything, will screw up.

On the way back, in Malton I go to an NHS dentist to see if I can get a broken tooth fixed. A harried receptionist says not to bother until next week, and then I'll have to pay. No, she doesn't have time to tell me how much.

Broken-toothed, de-Tigered, twenty four over par, I drive home past the achingly green fields doing the high harmonies on the Beatles and Penny Lane.

The Champions Trophy of Cricket starts tomorrow. Back home, I try to go on Ladbrokes to place a bet on South Africa, but nothing works. Customer support eventually tells me they "couldn't verify my age" so I have to send them a photograph of my passport!

De-betted too.

THURSDAY 1ST JUNE

THE TRUTH IS NOT A NICE GUY

I decide to do the Philip Larkin trail in Hull. For the drive, I search for Larkin poems on iTunes. There are none. Another audiobook opportunity.

Only the letters with Kingsley Amis, from the 1940s to the '80s, when Larkin died.

Friends from Oxford days, it is misogynist curmudgeonry of searing quality. Bad stuff is bum, and each signs off his letter with a bum reference as in Larkin's, *"Margaret Thatcher is noted for her head girl bum."*

The tour starts at the Royal Hotel. I have acquired from a jolly visitors' guide in the station the Philip Larkin Trail guide (free).

There are eleven spots around town where there are plaques containing excerpts of Larkin's writing. Apparently he didn't think much of Hull but it refuses to return the insult. Maybe he is just too famous, or notorious, depending on who you listen to. Perhaps, like the Beatles in Liverpool, he brings money to Hull.

In the bar, I order a shandy and a ploughman's lunch. I am in the same room Larkin wrote about. There are three single men, a threesome and a single woman, sitting so she can watch the platforms and the trains. She is raven-haired, has goth eye makeup and a sleeveless t-shirt. And a wedding ring.

A man leaves his keys on the bar. A girl from the threesome gets up and walks around one of the men, rubbing herself up against him like a cat.

I leave the bar and walk into Paragon Station where Larkin would catch the train to London, as in 'Whitsun Weddings'.

A few blocks away, I stroll under a repainted plaque of worn red brick reading 1535, behind a statue of Andrew Marvell. I am feeling moments of the eternal. Whose writing prevails over the centuries, and why?

Next, inside the entrance to Marks and Spencer's, next to the lift, a plaque quotes Larkin as saying, "I like to write about ordinary things". Like in 'The Large Cool Store'.

Larkin and Amis revel in disapproval. Not surprisingly Amis' wife eventually leaves him (from Amis to Larkin): "*...Glad to hear you're not entirely off the drink forever. Jane mentions that as her first condition for coming back to me. The second being that I presumably saw my head off and serve it up to her with a little hollandaise sauce.*"

I walk and I walk. There are people at the waterfront, the banks of the wide Humber. A tug chugs by at a snail's pace, its three crew a portrait in patience.

A chipboard wall is covered with a long frayed mural of the Nelson Mandela story. Students smoke up in the park.

Larkin represents the idea that you have to be very rude to tell the truth.

He reminds me of a certain kind of brilliant Englishman.

Fearfully well-educated, who use their intellect like a flamethrower, torching most things as "Boring!!", well-honed sarcasm about all and sundry. Usually their private lives are murky, as in the case of Amis and Larkin.

There's something hard nosed about the Yorkshire character, pessimistic, hard to impress, wounded by some insult of history.

Beauty surrounds you, but it's hard won.

THURSDAY 8TH JUNE
ELECTION MAYDAY

As part of Operation Cleanup and the arrival of the wyf, I take the car into a car wash in Malton. I had seen a sign for a price for five pounds. The car wash guy in a very thick accent (Polish) says, "Fifty".

"Fifty? Pounds??"

"Fifteen," says the guy on the driver's side. "His English no good."

Then a third guy sees the dog hairs and wet grass in the back and wants twenty. There's now five of them. Dark men with strong accents. Shrugging. Arms spread wide. In what? Supplication. Resignation.

"I just want my car washed. For fifteen pounds. Do fifteen pounds worth."

They stand there , agog.

"Okay?"

"Okay okay," the oldest guy says.

"How long?"

"Half an hour."

Back to the caravan, wash the bathroom. I hate doing this kind of thing. I need a walk. I chose from Geoff Brooks' Howardian Hills series Stearsby, Skewsby and Whenby, walk number 15. There's rain all around. I have to drive through a small lake across a rutted road to park my car up against a stone wall in Stearsby. Early on there's a beautiful lake in a wood. A grouse keeps darting ahead of me on the pathway, eventually taking flight and arcing around, almost skimming the wheat grasses as she flies and settles across the field.

Outside Stearsby, I meet a blowsy woman with an overbred spaniel. She just starts to chat. "Everyone's out today!"

(As if I were an old friend.)

"Did you vote?" She throws her scarf around her neck, a generous, expansive I-am-fearless kind of gesture.

"No, I'm a Canadian."

"Lucky. A Canadian who doesn't have to vote for either of these two fools."

"Did you do your patriotic duty?"

"Oh yes. And I live in hope."

(She voted for Theresa May, I'm sure.)

"What's a man from Canada doing here?"

"Well, I retired and I've moved here."

"Oh. What are you doing?"

"Nothing. Except writing a book." I regret it the moment it's out of my mouth.

"An exciting book, I hope."

"No. But I'm enjoying it."

"What's it about?"

Oh, I hate these revealing-everything-to-a-total-stranger-on-a- hillside conversations.

"Oh, it's about a wild guy who covers all these war zones and gets into all sorts of trouble."

"How very interesting."

"And what are you doing here?"

"My husband is retired from the foreign office. We live here but are about to move to the Dales. To be closer to ailing parents."

We bid each other farewell, she tossing her thick brown waves of hair against the wind and letting her dainty black and grey spaniel trot into the roadside grasses, snaffling happily away.

I wonder what her husband did 'in the foreign office'.

She is a swashbuckler, fun trouble on the diplomatic cocktail circuit, for sure. I wonder if he was a Scobie or that ambassador to Rwanda who backed the genocidaires.

Approaching Brandsby Hall, a second roadside encounter. An old man also in flat cap is walking towards me.

"Good afternoon. May I ask? Is Brandsby Hall open to the public?"

"No, it's private. New owners. Just a month ago." He waves at the fields. "You've noticed how the fields have shot up since the rain started just one week ago?" he asks.

"Yes." For a walker, the paths through the fields have become more difficult to negotiate because of the sudden growth.

His name is Geoff. "I'm eighty five."

"Can I ask you a question?"

"Yes, of course."

"Did you vote today?'

"No."

"What's the first election you remember?"

"I was born in 1932." He twists up his face and looks into the valley. "I can't remember."

"Eighty five." I do the math. 1932. Plus 13.

"Attlee. You must remember Attlee."

"And Churchill. Yesss."

He has a fixed smile, a sharp nose, a weathered face.

"Churchill won the war and lost the election," he says.

"A shocker."

He laughs, and then, serious. "My brother was in the second war, my father in the first."

"You were too young?"

"I went to register but I was a farmworker so they sent me back."

"To this village?"

"Yes." His mind changes direction suddenly. "There was a lawyer from York. Or from London." He seems to struggle remembering. "From London, yes, and my father bought seventeen acres off him. Managed to find the money. Then later I made it into twenty five. Raised red beets, potatoes, some wheat, a few sheep, some cattle. It was hard work though. I should have let out some of the land, y'know."

He chuckles as if I understood intimately the foolish choices we all make.

"Well, you're eighty five, you're walking, you look to me like you're in pretty good nick."

"My doctor says I should keep active. So I cut the grass."

"Up and about is best."

We stand there at the side of the road outside Brandsby Hall with our walking sticks and flat caps.

"Okay, Geoff," I say. I am trying to leave now, but the old farmworker, like the Ancient Mariner, wants to hold me.

"It gets pretty windy and stormy now around here now."

"Well, I'm from Canada. The winters there are brutal. Snow and ice four months of the year. I'll take this anytime. Golfed in February."

"You don't see snow around here anymore. This is Brandsby." He turns around. "Next village is Stearsby, Skewsby, Whenby, then further up and around the hill is Danby. There was a couple up there, it was 1946, they had a market stall in York. They couldn't go for six weeks. They were shut in. The snow was as high as the hedges. Well, they cut them down in those days, half the height of what they are now."

"Global warming?"

He looks away, then back, fixing my eye. "When I was a boy, the summers were hotter. I think. Real summer days. Now it's windy with storms."

"Mmmm. Okay, Geoff, I should get going."

"Okay."

"Nice talking to you."

"Yes, very nice."

We shake hands, his a skeleton soon to be de-fleshed.

Returning to the car, I try a shortcut through a farmer's field. At one point, I get a good nettling. I've been stung before by nettles in Canada and South Africa but these ones make my legs hum for hours. A dull numb stinging surface ache. It feels like a higher form of vegetable venom. I have another wobble trying to stay ahead of a herd of over-inquisitive black cattle down an extremely muddy slope. Just the day before, I'd read in the newspaper about the demise of a wealthy inventor, trampled to death in Sussex by a herd of cows. Bulls I must be afraid of but I'm not aware that cows can kill. I must look into this as I clear the field by clambering over a large metal fence. The inventor had been an Oxford medical technology man who had invented needle-free injections. A medical company paid him five hundred and forty two million pounds. He was eighty… had everything, the pot of gold, could afford to do anything in the world that money can buy, and he is trampled to death by a herd of cows in Sussex, *going for a walk*.

Four hours later my legs are still singing.

I take a nap, because I expect a long night of election watching. When I wake, I watch Eggheads, and the third episode of Paula, a fine drama with an impossible ending. Shortly before ten, I tune into the BBC for election coverage which will last until one pm the next day.

Background. Everyone expects May to win a majority. Setting aside my leftish bias, I note Corbyn's authenticity and how hugely biased all the British media seemed to be, against him. I decide to put a fiver on May not getting a majority at 16-1.

It is one of the most fascinating political processes of my life, this election campaign, studded by three terror attacks, the second at the Manchester Arena quite unprecedented in what it targets. It's been very intense. Both main parties issue manifestoes. Corbyn's is daring and brilliant. Big strokes.

Nick the tax-avoiding rich to pay for NHS, schooling and free university for all who qualify. He will immediately legalise EU nationals in the UK. It's as if he's stolen Justin Trudeau's winning trifecta. The youth, immigrants and new voters. He dives into adoring crowds, connects with people, answers questions with conviction. On the other hand, May shows all the stress of an expensive wound-up doll, defending typical Tory indefensibles with robotic clichés. How many times does one have to say "I am Strong and Stable" before people wonder why you have to repeat it, time and time again. She avoids general crowds, going with clutches of dry supporters at photo-ops. Whoever Theresa May really is, they aren't letting her out of the tailored suits.

So at ten, David Dimbleby releases the results of the BBC/ITV/Sky exit poll. The official polls will not yield results for two, three four hours. Not until four or five in the morning! In North America, it's over in a matter of an hour or two, with networks competing with each other to declare the winner first. Here, with unbelievably intelligent digital technology, the process unfolds in great detail with remote reporters all over the place. And significance, and heartbreak. And tremendous nervousness about the accuracy of the exit polls which, as I understand it, sample voters as they leave a hundred and twenty-odd polling stations.

One hundred and twenty out of what? Thousands. One of the panellists is the man who runs the BBC exit poll system and after several hours, he is able to say that his exit polls have been very accurate. It is extraordinarily close to the final tally.

May looks shell-shocked as the votes are tallied at her constituency in Kent but she is then cocooned with advisers and they scurry her off to the Palace where the Firm does its nodding job to buttress the Tory's tenuous hold on power. The momentum is with Corbyn and, at this moment, seems destined for Number Ten, but May and her gang will hang on to power as desperate elites have done throughout history. The battle may have been lost but Labour seems to have won the war.

It's as gripping and as profound as electoral politics can get.

Terrific television.

SATURDAY 10TH JUNE

REDBEARD AT BAT

Today I umpire my second game for Sheriff Hutton CC, and I think I have been accepted.

People who know me will know my abiding passion for cricket.

As a seventeen year old in South Africa, I was a very good player at a time of the golden generation of South African cricketers, but apartheid, to make things short, intervened and I was removed from the country, ending up in Canada. I will never know what might have happened to my cricket career. In Canada, after eight years of not playing, I joined a club in Toronto and loved the thirty years I played the game in village-level cricket there.

Now my Canadian life is past. After fifty seven years away, I am back in England, and not only England, but its cricketing crucible, the county of Yorkshire. At sixty six, my age doesn't allow me to play with confidence anymore, but one of my intentions is to volunteer with a local village club as an umpire. My first two attempts, at Hovingham and Slingsby yield nothing, but on the internet I find a local club that advertises for volunteers. I call them up and one thing leads to another. Last Wednesday I took to the field at Sheriff Hutton with its ruined eight hundred year old castle just south of the ground. It was a twenty over game.

I am not going to try and explain cricket to the innocent. It's complicated. Like many arcane sports, one has to be raised in the game to understand its soul and essence. It's a behaviour as much as a game. Eleven players on both sides. One side bats and tries to accumulate as many runs as possible in an allotted number of six-ball overs. The other side fields and tries to bowl the batting side out for as few runs as possible.

The umpire is asked, often loudly in the form of the word "Howzat?" (how is that?) whether a batsman is out and he makes his decision. If out, he raises his finger into the air.

The key to umpiring is to be invisible. To be effectively invisible, one must know the game intimately. Beyond calling the end of each six-ball over, one has to watch for no-balls, wides, snicks, byes and leg byes, boundaries, stumpings, run-outs, short runs, and half a dozen other cricketing oddities. If one does that and has the requisite seriousness, the players respect you and forget about you, and it's quite simple. I learned from a book by the greatest Yorkshire umpire ever, Dickie Bird, that one also has to be genial, but unwavering.

After the first game on Wednesday, the players all

thanked me and asked me back for the big test, the 1st XI match today, Saturday.

The quality of the cricket is quite good. The balance of restraint and intensity is perfect.

I had written to my dear Uncle Alan a few days back, the most English person I know, and he signed off his reply by saying, "don't worry about the umpiring, you have the requisite gravitas."

The first six overs of today's game are tight. The two opening bowlers are accurate, fast and the two opening batsmen defend skilfully. Only eleven runs are on the board when I have a National Geographic moment. The Yorkshire wind is blowing low grey clouds across the sky behind the rotund red-bearded right hander at bat before me. The young springy fast bowler at my end is moving the ball away off the seam on off stump. One has the feeling that something is about to give. As I hear the bowler's footfalls approach from behind, Red Beard the batsman clenches his jaw, narrows his eyes and sinks six inches lower in his stance, pounding his bat into his mark. The wicketkeeper and slip lean forward in anticipation and SNAPPP. It is one of those images of perfection in one's life. Everything comes to a total stop. Freeze frame. Being exactly where one wants to be, where one should be, after decades of being in a place that never completely fit.

In the bigger picture, this moment is trivial. Theresa May, Manchester, Trump, the disappearance of the anchovy run off Peru, Syria. And it *is* far away from all that. Insulated. North Yorkshire re-voted Conservative yesterday. It's an agricultural place. It's a heavenly place. I walk miles alone in an English paradise. I am not responsible for it. I am not responsible. I have turned away from the battle, unexpectedly even to myself. I was so engaged. So into everything. Pushing, elbowing, with an agenda. Change, liberalism, knocking out opponents, stalking powerful fossils.

For many years, people wanted my work. People wanted to hear what I had to say. Mandela is The Man. Tax thieves are draining the lifeblood out of nations. America is a dangerous disappointment. They lost interest. The passions of decades-long idealism became the ravings of an increasingly cranky older man. I was in danger of becoming unpleasant. It was time either to up the battle, or walk away. I had to remind myself that my windmills are not their windmills. And nobody is going to pay to watch me tilt at yesterday's shibboleths. I had to admit defeat. There's nothing worse than an old fighter stumbling into the ring, chasing past glories. I stunned myself and a few others by shutting it all down. But mostly the decision-makers lost interest. I walked away. Now I am drawn to becoming invisible, disempowered, completely neutral. An Umpire in North Yorkshire.

Like the ruined castle behind the cricket ground, nature will assume its sovereignty.

The ball is delivered and the film restarts.

Two balls later, as is the way with cricket, something bizarre and loud suddenly happens. Red Beard explodes out his crouch and crushes a short ball directly off the meat of his bat at my chest twenty two yards away. Instinctively my trunk starts to spin away, but the bowler manages to put two fingers on the ball, skewing it at speed into the stumps at the bowler's end, right in front of me. My eyes swivel in a nanosecond to the batsman at the non-striker's end, and he has screwed his left boot back over the line just in time. There's a tremendous appeal, answered immediately by my certain and clear, "NOT OUT".

There's a silence. Everyone knows I've got it right.

Respect is won. Play continues. It is a dismissal that happens rarely, but it is out if the batsman at the bowler's end is backing up properly, anticipating a run. A ball hit back at that speed, deflected so slightly and accurately, invariably results in the non-striker being out of his ground and out, run out. But he isn't. I feel vindicated that my cricketing muscle memory is intact after forty seven years.

It turns out that the visiting team has only five of their usual batsmen and the rest are school kids from their village. As each successive batsman comes to the crease, they seem to get shorter and younger. Batting at number 9 is a bony boy called Ben. He can't be much older than his number in the batting line-up. The top of the stumps is level with his ribs. But the local team is ruthless. They keep their best bowlers on, somewhat mercilessly. The nippy lefthander from the other end has six wickets and wants to break his record of eight in an innings. Also they want a result before the rains come. But Ben holds out. His technique and fortitude is laudable. At one point, a very good off cutter from the lefty leaps off the pitch and hits him in the heart. Now normally in any cricket I have played where kids are involved, one a) brings on the slowest bowler, to avoid this kind of danger, but if it happens b) rushes up to the stricken kid immediately. But these are Yorkshiremen. The bowler turns away for the last ball of his spell as if nothing untoward has happened. I delay this by walking in from square leg, asking the kid quite clearly so they can all hear, "Are you alright?"

Ben does not interrupt taking his guard, but does turn his head sharply towards me.

The look he gives me is admonishing, as if I am a soft-in-tha-'ead foreigner interrupting a tribal rite. His look sends me right back to my place. The elderly batsman, the last one, the man at the other end says in a very strong accent, "Don't let them see you touch it, lad."

I had misread. Never show them fear. The Yorkshire way. Real cricket. Toughness as a virtue. Ben defends the last ball beautifully, balance forward, head over the ball, elbow up. The bowler continues his run-up to pat the kid on the head. Like he'd passed the test. The villagers watching give him earned applause.

When they bat, the two burly twenty-something Sheriff Hutton openers knock off the runs just as the rains come in.

It's been an intriguing gem of a game. I am totally into every single ball.

In the dressing room they thank me profusely.

"Will ya stay for tea?"

"My wife just flew in from Canada. I have to go."

They are perplexed as if I have just said something in Martian.

"Six thirty Wednesday then?" two of them say, in unison.

"See you then."

SUNDAY 11TH JUNE

THE PAINTER, THE POTTER AND THE PROMISE-MAKER

"One thing leads to another leads to another," I am saying to the painter who owns a horse farm. "You meet someone who leads to an event where you meet someone who leads you here."

She understands perfectly.

The day starts with Nicky and I sleeping in a bit before heading off to Malton for a traditional English breakfast. We drop into the Malton News, pick up an Observer and the proprietor points down the street to the Yorkshire Tea Room, a trio of rooms in an old building beyond the traffic light that has heretofore eluded me.

It's perfect. The articles in the paper are brilliant, dominated by post mortems on the election shocker. It is extraordinary to me how the coverage is so blindingly uncritical of May and critical of Corbyn until the mainstream media reluctantly recognises what is obvious to my eyes. The crowds for Corbyn are organic, large, and in the case of young people, increasingly adoring. On the other hand, May speaks woodenly before the Tory faithful in carefully predesigned photo-ops. Someone must have gone to such detail to plan it all. The smiling factory managers and the leader. The leader tours the Summerland crèche today. Tomorrow, she visits such and such community centre, or school, though not too much of that.

The numbers require her to form an alliance with a small Northern Ireland party to stay in power. A piece about the DUP catches the eye. By an academic who has written a book about them. Apparently they grew out of a tiny Protestant church founded by the fanatical Ian Paisley, and are fiercely anti-Catholic. More than fifty percent of their members would have a problem with their children marrying a Catholic. They are anti-abortion and anti-gay marriage. Apparently May and her Tory cabal are quite liberal on social policy. How desperate does one become to keep power? What a scenario.

Labour plans a radical program and preparation for another general election within the year. Corbyn is interviewed and is witty, serious and totally on top of the details and the process ahead.

The stakes are very high. People who oppose Brexit now have hope.

All fascinating stuff, pushing the awful Trump who surely is even more a candidate for ousting. As for the rest of the world, barely a mention. (The late news reports that the Manchester bomber built the explosive entirely himself and that there is not a sinister network behind him, as so many said when it happened. This is even less reassuring.)

On our way to the breakfast cafe we spot a little yellow sign pointing up one of those old alleys: North Yorkshire Open Studios. After breakfast, we decide at the last minute to pop in. It is an engraver, a woman who makes plant studies of the utmost detail and delicacy. She walks me through the kinds of wood she uses, her carving tools with all their different names and thicknesses of blade, the fact that she holds and carves in a pinched shallow manner so the scour is no deeper than it needs to be. We ask if there are other artists on show and she directs us back to the newsagent, who has free copies of the Open Studios' programme on the window shelf. Nicky stays behind and negotiates to buy a couple of small prints. As I wait in the sunshine, an elderly woman is leaving. I see an opportunity I always like to take. Loneliness. I may be wrong but I sense loneliness. She is wearing a lovely floral jacket, soft violets, and blues, big heady flowers on white.

"Now if I may say," waiting until she gives me her full attention, "that is a really lovely jacket."

She beams.

"Why, thank you."

"This is a lovely idea, these open studios. Are there any others close by?"

"Oh yes. Just outside of Norton. Up the Beverley Road. There are two of them. A painter and a potter. At the Highfield Racing Stables. You know you are in horse country?"

"Yes. We'll have a look. Thank you."

The Racing Stables turn out to be the neatest I've seen. The grass verges and hedges are tightly clipped, nothing lies on the ground. We take a wrong turn in the stables and walk past a succession of beautiful young racehorses, most them lying down, sleeping, presumably after rigorous morning workouts. We double back and spot a yellow arrow pointing upstairs. A woman with a paint-splattered shirt greets us. The paintings of Catriona Stewart are what I would describe as bold primitive, Big Ideas. Paradise Lost. Male and Female. Not a refined, educated technique but bold and interesting. She is a great character and owns the farm. The other artist, Jill Ford, throws vases and I covet a dish with tiny perforations and a bent lip, which Nicky decides to buy, as well as a small metallic glazed dish for herself. But we didn't have enough money. So I drive back to Norton to the nearest cashpoint. By the time I get back, Nicky has found out that Jill knows her energy medicine teacher. They are also into wild swimming.

They mention the farm is a famous stable leased by a trainer called Quinn. Catriona is asking us over for dinner and is planning swimming outings. I ask her for a recommendation for a nearby hike. She looks down, puts her finger to her mouth and thinks.

"Thixendale. You need to go to Thixendale. It's a

valley," making a valley shape with her arms, "with all sorts of paths and trails."

So, after a winding ten minute drive, we find ourselves drifting around this exquisite valley on ageworn shale roads surrounded by wheat and grasslands that ripple and wave in the wind. We see hares, a vast winged owl, all sorts of twittering and tweeting birds and after an hour and forty minutes swing through an abandoned farmyard with a World War Two soldier-mannequin in a doorway keeping guard… initially a chilling effect.

Home to the cricket and the most appalling collapse in South Africa's history. Just awful. But it doesn't matter. There are other things in life. But if one is only a fanatic lover of the South African cricket team one would be tempted to cut one's throat.

Later both AB De Villiers and Theresa May maintain a stiff upper lip. They do not consider themselves in any kind of trouble.

Must be the Age of the Deniers.

MONDAY 12TH JUNE

HOPES AND DREAMS

I am sitting in the cafeteria of the Redcar Library in Middlesbrough, waiting for the start of the self-publishing workshop session of the Stockton on Tees literary festival. It's an open community library, semi-modern, part of a '60s complex built in the ruins of a rust belt port. Ordinary folks wait in line. I ask the librarian, a brown haired woman with glasses, where the self-publishing session is. She walks me over to the open door. There's a cafeteria. I buy a coffee and search the name of the company, Sixth Element Publishing. It features an author who has written a book on Middlesbrough FC. I see a few people sitting in a side room where the session is to take place.

It starts in ten minutes so I'll go in now.

The workshop is led by a diminutive red-haired lady and her business partner, a dark haired good-looking man with lots of tattoos, who does the graphics, layout and covers.

On one page she lists the topics she will cover. The language is plain, as is her style. They offer author's services. They will mentor, edit, and publish the book. They have several examples. Children's books, travel books, science fiction, crime, romance, and they seem well produced. They care about the font, the paper, the dimensions. I like them. They are sincere, frank.

There are about eighteen people on plastic chairs in a circle. Each one introduces him or herself, and what they are working on. They range from thirty to seventy. Most are women, over fifty.

They feel like readers. Novels, poems, science fiction, murder mysteries. One woman introduces herself by saying, laughing deliciously, "I've thought about one hundred ways to kill someone."

Another woman, who seems like a proud angel, wounded from a hippie life gone bad, declares with a nervous waver in her voice, "I have written a novel about the lives of five woman." The way she says it, her tentative strength, makes me want to read it.

The man to my right, he looks like a retired maths teacher, has written a book about two lads who grew up in Boro together, drifted apart, lived completely different lives and then came back together again. Ditto. The woman to my left has the most beautiful colouring, very light chocolate, announces herself in a strong Spanish accent as Peruvian. She has Incan rings on her toes and fingers, and is writing a book on Peruvian recipes. At the end I tell her I did a documentary about cocaine guerrillas in Peru in the 1990s.

"Peru has changed since then," she says. "It has changed a lot," and even later I say, "I love the ceviche in Peru. And the Pisco Sours."

I meant to catch her afterwards and tell her about my Rategan story in Peru with a view of sending it to her. But I got delayed by the host, trying to thank her.

The thing about these participants that, as a friend puts it, "it was a room full of hope".

"And dreams too," I add.

I love that. I love their wispy story ideas, their body language, their accents, their inquisitiveness, their humour, the life therein.

A black girl arrives late, perhaps Ethiopian originally, or through her parents, or a parent. Slender, thick dark hair, wearing jeans and a brightly coloured vest over her shirt.

And I think, that's the sort of Briton who lives in the projects, has a child, struggles, but has a dream, a novel she's been writing for years, one which will win her The Booker and make her one of the nation's most celebrated voices, a story, and further stories that will enable her to give her son or daughter enough to give him or her a chance, happiness, security, expression. Freedom of expression, freedom from fear, freedom from persecution because of her gender.

TUESDAY 13TH JUNE

THE BETRAYED VILLAGE

What a day.

Randomly, I decide we will do one of Britain's best coastal walks, as recommended by The Observer and Julia.

From Old Saltburn to Warsett.

It takes more than an hour to get there. We stop at Kirkbymoorside for a cappuccino and carrot cake. The Moors road is fringed with sheep.

The weather is slightly overcast, not windy. The panoramic views are breathtaking. We bump into two girlfriends with their dogs and ask how long it takes.

"Depends how much we are nattering," and then dissolve into hysterics.

We have Sophie with us. Very low maintenance French beagle.

We come across an air shaft and are told by two other women hikers that it was used to air out iron mines.

Beneath us warrens. Dads, mums and kids laboured thereunder. Never do find Warsett but descend to the beach, and are told a small village dwells in the cleft.

"Oh boy. I could really do with some fish and chips. Wouldn't it be nice if we came into the village and there was Amy's Fish and Chips, right there."

We come into the village which at first appears to be shacks on a hillside, gypsy shacks, I think. There is an old open fishing boat with strong wooden sculptures of a fisherman in the prow and the stern, absolutely perfectly angled into the imagined headwind and swell, and there, lo and behold, Skinningrove Fish and Chips. White lettering on a closed back sliding door. Oh well.

We walk past the edge of it and there it is. An open fish and chip shop. Tracy runs it, a third generation Skinningrovist. She's happy to whip up the cod in batter and chips for us as she is just closing and they are the last pieces.

"Are there still fishermen?" I ask.

"Oh yes. My husband is a fisherman. We own three boats in Whitby and Saltburn."

"Better harbours, huh?"

"Yes."

"Lots of early mornings," I say.

She laughs, blonde hair, lots of laughter wrinkles, nice strong local accent.

"If I may ask, do you have children?"

"Three sons, all grown up, all at sea. Five grandchildren."

"Five grandchildren? What ages?"

"Eight, seven, six, three and two months."

"That would be quite a handful all at once."

"Sometimes when I'm finished a full day here, I have them over and I'm really tired."

"Knackered," I say. I love 'knackered', the word, using it whenever I get the chance. It's one of the words that makes me feel more English than I am.

"Exactly," she nods, the fish crackling in the oil.

"If I may say, you look way too young to have five grandchildren."

She laughs bashfully. It's true. Behind me, Nicky laughs, knowing my silver tongued ways.

"Do you get some big winds here?"

"Oh yes. And bad flooding. The river. I was four feet under in my house. Five weeks ago. The fire brigade came in the middle of the night."

"I guess that did the carpets."

"Definitely."

"Did you have insurance?"

"Oh yes, the insurance was good."

"But your rates went up?" asks Nicky.

"Oh yes."

"Do you think it was global warming," N asks.

"Oh yes, definitely."

She serves us. We are the only customers. A small room, three tables. The Dog, looped up outside, whines occasionally.

"What's the population here?"

"258."

"Is there a school?"

"Oh yes, primary, up the road."

"What are those shacks on the hill?"

"Pigeon coops. Racing Pigeons. It's very big here. Goes back as long as I can remember."

"Interesting. How does that work?"

"They come and gather the pigeons and take them to France or Spain, even as far as America, let them go and the first one back wins. There's lots of money involved."

"That sounds like a documentary," I say.

"Maybe. My grandfather raced pigeons. He'd show me them as a special treat but I had to be absolutely quiet."

I imagine the mystery and tensions and specialness of a little blonde girl circa 1960 going to the cooing coop with grandpa, maybe a lantern, the sounds of the sea and the wind.

We devour the fish, which is melt-in-your-mouth flaky. I think of asking what's the secret to her batter, light and crispy and evenly coating, but pass. Whew. It's far and away the best fish and chips I've ever eaten, but I'm no expert.

We ask if we can get a taxi back. She has a number and takes care of it. She's cleaning up now and we are outside waiting for the taxi. Nine pounds all the way back, including two pounds for the dog.

"I'm just going to have a fag while we wait," she says, stepping outside and locking up. "Yes, this village has a lot of stories. See those flats." Pointing across the way to a two storey rundown building. "That used to be a hospital. In the war they'd move the patients into the caves across the river. Come here." She takes me round the side between two boat shacks. There's the river. In the bank on the other side, three cave mouths. "There used to be a bridge across."

"Germans bombed along here?" (Realising only later that of course Middlesbrough and those industrial centres and the ports would be a big target for the Luftwaffe. Big steel and iron production centre.) I imagine the bodies on stretchers being run across the bridge into the caves with some gerry-rigged siren wailing away in the night.

I glance up at the pigeon shacks against the horizon and think. One reason they are based here is because there is no smog or city lights to distract them on the final, critical sprint home. They must have digital transmitters on them now, and the owners and punters can probably track them online. Blip. Gone. Somewhere over the Atlantic. I bet they have names like Mercury Wing, or Lightning Jack. Maybe not lightning. Asking for trouble. How big are their lungs, I am thinking. How fast must their little hearts pound? And of course, how do they find their way home? Incredible. Nature webbed to man's lust to win. And the money. It's a movie. Been done no doubt.

As we walk back, she says, "And then there's the Merman. The legend."

"The legend of the Merman? What a village."

We go back to finish our tea.

I confess to her, she has given so much in such a short period of time. "I actually am a documentary filmmaker and I would be interested in speaking to the top pigeon racer in the village."

"That would be my neighbour, Dave."

We exchange phone numbers. She spots someone across the street, a woman having a smoke in her tiny garden, dressed in pink house clothes.

"Mickey, who's a big pigeon man?"

"Who wants to know?"

"Here's a filmmaker fella from… where are ya from?"

"Canada."

" 'E's from Canada. 'E wants to speak to one of the pigeon fellas."

"Oooh let me think."

"There's me neighbour."

"Oooh Dave 'e'd be good, but Staffy."

"Staffy'd be perfect."

"Lives for 'is birds 'e does."

"Staffy'd be perfect for you."

"I got yer number. I'll call yer in two days time. Ask 'em if I can talk to 'em about a big pigeon race," I say.

"Will do."

She takes a drag of her cig.

"We all have nicknames… she's Mickey, but her real name's Sue."

"What are you?" Nicky asks.

"Gingertop," and explodes with laughter. Bad teeth. No mind. She goes quiet, then.

"But we've had a documentary done on Skinningrove."

"Really?"

"It was dead awful. They spoke to all the worst characters in village. Made us look terrible."

"Which channel?

"Channel 4. Britain's Worst Villages."

"Did they tell you they were going to do that?"

"No-no-no. They said they were doing summat about British villages. I run a youth group, I volunteer. Fella came to me and said something about wanting to show something positive about what young people do in the village. They came and filmed for a whole day and a half. Interviewed me for a long time. I put in a good word for them at the council."

"Didn't use any of it?" says Nicky.

"Not a bit."

Nodding to me, Nicky says, "Well, he wouldn't do that."

But I know. Once bitten, twice shy.

The taxi rolls up.

Tracy is her real name. Lovely lovely person.

We bid fond farewells. I say I'll call but I can't see it happening. I'm retired from that anyway.

Back at the caravan I google the Channel Four documentary. It's treachery. Britain's roughest villages. They actually interview a retarded boy by the river.

"I was born in toilet," he says. "Me ma dropped me into the toilet, and somebody said git 'im outta there, he'll drown."

Lots of posed shots, a torn shirt in the middle of the

road, a car wreck, doom music. Long shots in dreary miserable weather. Shots of poor people. Nauseating.

I think I could make this place look as beautiful as I find it, just as they made it look like some retard hellhole of threatening morons.

"Imagine the national humiliation," Nicky says.

WEDNESDAY 14TH JUNE
LUCKY CHARM

Golf. The Clutch. About fifteen retired gents participate twice a week in the Clutch. Couple of pounds in, lowest net twosome wins, and birdies win. Barry Moment, a retired firefighter, Tony born in Birmingham and Mark the field hockey player and I win. I birdie the par three seventeenth for five pounds and take six pounds on top of that. It's another beautiful day. Nice wind coming down the valley to the sea. At the end, in the bar, Barry says, "Come and sit with us, Robin, we want you to feel that you are one of us."

Then into a rough street in Scarborough to pick up winnings from betting on Corbyn.

Then home for a shower and a nap before six o'clock umpiring Sheriff Hutton v Alne. The boys play well.

Give four outs including a clipped bail from square leg their dopey umpire misses.

The sky becomes filled with a massive high table of vapour. The castle is ruined to the point of dangerous precariousness. One wing of it seems to totter on a few bricks waiting to be blown over and onto the heads of tourists.

Sheriff Hutton CC wins and the skipper says, "That's two in a row. Robin is our lucky charm."

FRIDAY 16TH JUNE

CITIZEN CLEM AND THE CONSORTIUM

I get up, do my Pilates, shower, have my granola and strawberries, and drive into Malton. Nick has bought a fifty pound chair at a charity shop but I have to kill an hour before I can pick it up so I take the Guardian to Costa and have a cappuccino and read about the recent Grenfell Tower fire, its aftermath and everything else. Theresa May visits the firefighters but not any victims. Corbyn does both, embracing the victims. He is already father of the nation. An editorial stingingly declares Grenfell May's Katrina. Bullseye.

There is also an excellent accountability chart of the companies and executives responsible for the cladding and dangerous conditions at Grenfell.

Also John Bew, who wrote Citizen Clem, the excellent biography of Clement Attlee wins the Orwell prize, and the judges lavish praise on the book. Corbyn as the new Attlee is declared. But there are several big differences. Attlee was a big patriot, a public school idealist, an

Oxbridge graduate, and a war hero (Mesopotamia and Gallipoli). He was also Mayor of Stepney, in London's East End. Corbyn may not be as patriotic, although that is a less revered quality today. He is a college dropout. He's never been in the military or combat of any sort. And he went to a regular high school.

But his manifesto is very Attlee, nationalisation, free education and child care, and he has a similarity that I think is critical. He is not a media hog. He understands that things have to get done by a team. He eschews individuality, unlike the Churchills and the Mays. Vote for me, is replaced by, read this (holding the manifesto up). Vote for it, vote for us.

There is also a very interesting piece about the American take on Corbyn. At first, US commentators are dismissive and anecdotal. "Friend of Hamas, peacenik." Now they are very concerned to the point of hostility. Corbyn, they say, is not a strong ally or "someone we can trust".

The Hamas thing is particularly interesting. The Israel lobby takes no prisoners. Humanise the Palestinians, and you are an anti-semite.

They understand well that if centre-left principles of democracy and human rights are applied, the Israeli right, the apartheid reflex and its zealots, must fight it. On every front, clean and dirty. But they do not accept democracy. To be a democrat, one is anti-Israel, ergo an anti-semite. It doesn't mean one does not respect the horrors of the holocaust and the rights of Israel and Israelis. I believe business and the Israel lobby will be doing their utmost to keep Corbyn from taking the power that seems to be very much within his grasp.

He has grown enormously since the beginning of the election when he was seen as a completely flaky loser, even by many in his own party and by eighty percent of the mainstream media.

The Grenfell Tower catastrophe highlights the apartheid nature of London society. Almost all of the victims are of colour, many Moslems. And they lived amidst some of the wealthiest individuals and expensive real estate in the world, in Kensington. It's Hillbrow in Sandton (Johannesburg), Regent Park in Rosedale (Toronto).

Simon Cowell, the reality show blowhard, announces he will record a single and donate the proceeds to a victims' fund. He and that Piers Morgan character. The new David Frosts, maybe worse.

The sports news is that Ronaldo wants to quit Spain one year into his five-year deal with Real Madrid because he is insulted by allegations of tax evasion! And Everton has solved its goalie problem by signing an English kid for thirty million pounds.

To kill ten more minutes in Costa, I take the free copy of the Daily Mail and read there about the wealth of the owners of the company that runs the Tower and the sub-contractor that did the cladding. Multi-million dollar homes, Porsches, ski and safari holidays and "no comment" at the doorstep. The death toll could climb to seventy.

For the walk, I have Rievaulx Abbey in mind and drive through Helmsley, which is thick with black-leathered bikers. I walk for one and a half hours out, past the most beautiful cottage at Rievaulx Bridge, as what looks like a World War Two fighter plane flies over my head. It must be the best engine sound in the world. On past the most lovely pools that look perfect for trout fishing, fringed by an energetically bubbling brook, up a hillside chalk road between towering evergreens. I climb out to a village called Cold Kirkby, as a mizzle sweeps through and reveals a freshly washed North Yorkshire panorama with two big-bellied helicopter gunships crossing the sky like slightly ominous bumble bees, way off in the distance. I imagine sending a letter to the RAF base saying how much I have enjoyed the blissful peace of the North Yorkshire Moors and Wolds, "apart from your infernal war machines spoiling paradise, reminding me of the terrible times in which we live", but I know it would be binned, or at best, prompt a form letter.

"Another bloody tree-hugger, flight."

I keep hearing gun reports but it turns out to be those scare guns in the fields, keeping various avian raiders at bay.

On the way down I encounter a man with very expensive fly-fishing gear, heading for the pools.

"Are these pools fishable?" I ask.

"Well, not exactly. They are a privately held by a consortium."

"I'm from Canada. Does one need a license to fish in rivers here?"

"Yes. There's a shop in Thirsk that can help you. It's the gun shop there."

He is money. He is perfectly turned out. The hat, the trout man's vest, the tightly trimmed moustache and sideburns. There is just the slightest hint of impatience, barely detectable, but if I ask one more question it will reveal itself.

"Well, thank you very much… good luck."

At the bottom of the path, there is a gleaming silver Range Rover which is about as far from a Jeep as a car can get. Private v Public again.

THURSDAY 22ND JUNE

"WITHIN YOUR GOLFING BUDGET"

Way back in February, when I was scouting local golf courses, I came across Ganton. It's the posh, expensive course in the neighbourhood. I went and played it, for fifty five quid. The six time Open winner Harry Vardon was the professional here more than a century ago. It's a onetime Ryder Cup course (1949) and lauds itself as being one of the top eighty golf courses in the world. (One assumes it's ranked somewhere in the seventies). In December of last year, the Secretary emailed suggesting I apply to be an overseas member for three hundred and forty eight pounds a year. To join as a full member involves a waiting list of two and a half years and something like thirty five thousand pounds. It will teach me a lesson about the different meaning of the word secretary in Britain. A secretary elsewhere in the world is an outdated and often sexist term for an assistant to the boss. Not here. In the world of Yorkshire Golf, the Secretary wields some power, it seems. But it's not as simple as paying the money, writes the Secretary. A background letter is required, which I provide reluctantly. I'm less of Old Etonian CEO millionaire than a broke-ass documentary filmmaker, as my son once described me. Albeit a fearless golf nut. And as Jim Carrey told me in an interview, "I don't mind you asking some questions but you don't have to know the label on my underwear."

Three months later, just before I leave for Ireland, I get a call from the Chairman of the membership committee, let's call him the Banker. He says the membership committee is meeting to discuss my application and when can I play an "introductory round?" After I get back from Ireland. He says he'll "move it along".

On my return there's no contact. I go and play the course again, this time gagging on the full visitors' rate of eighty five pounds. Most of the greens are out of service. When I ask in the pro shop if I can get a discount, a grim-faced assistant looks at me as if I have just farted. After the round I pop in to see the Secretary. A polite RAF man, let's call him Two-Names. He tells me there's been "new elections" and that the new Chairman of the membership sub-committee, no longer The Banker, will be in touch.

What is this? The Angolan Politburo? My anti-snobbery instincts are flaring.

As a course, it is interesting. Mostly flat with the odd undulation, its fairways and greens are nicely grassed and cut. It features a few longish par fours and a lot of deep bunkers filled with a cloddish, heavy, brown soil. Clearly the Ganton members, predominantly geriatric, feel themselves to be a cut above the general mob who play golf in Yorkshire. Despite assurances that the new head of the membership sub-committee will be contacting me about my introductory round, he never does. Months after the initial email exchange, and well into the season, I have given up on them and joined Scarborough South Cliff. For my taste, with its spectacular cliffside views of the North Sea, a more attractive course, same price, and more agreeable staff and members.

Some five months after the initial offer from the club, and against my better judgement, I send another email to Two-Names. No reply. I read a blog entry on Ganton from a disgruntled American saying they're happy to take your money but are unhelpful. To cut a long story short, Banker does eventually call, apparently now restored to the chairmanship of the membership sub-committee, and the promised golf outing is booked in June. The night before, I get a phone message from my host which advises me bring jacket and tie, for a post-round meeting, neither of which I have brought to Yorkshire. My bad. Early next morning I go into Malton early to drop my wife off at the station for her trip to London and her performance of 'Hooked' at the Royal Academy of Dramatic Art. My tee-off is booked for nine, so there I am at seven thirty in the morning scouring Malton for a tie. Eventually I unearth a revolting little three pound black curtain material number in ASDA. I then realise I have forgotten my jacket at home and have to whip back there. Just hanging the jacket in the car, I notice a hole visible below the left pocket. Woe is me. I rush to the course and meet The Banker who is the Chairman of the committee that he was no longer Chairman of, and his two playing companions. We'll call them Grumps and Carver, a surgeon. We tee off an hour after I had been told. The round is okay. The banker guy is a super golfer, about an 8. I am as charming as I can be, but feel it is a lost cause. My unease is stirred by their intrusive queries, clearly intended to gauge my true residency and my financial worth. Unacceptably nosy. It's just a game of golf. I don't think one should discuss money, politics or religion on a first round with strangers. Probably never. Golf is an escape. These ruling class Yorkshiremen are laying it on too thick for my comfort. I didn't feel socially comfortable with them, and probably not they with me.

At one point, one of them castigates the Chairman about the new bunker rakes the club has acquired.

"They are absolutely hopeless. They're curved at the ends. They don't give an even rake. At the ends, the grooves are too deep."

The Banker notes, "The ladies have been complaining too."

"What's their problem?" says Grumps.

'They say they are too heavy."

"And misshapen," says the Carver the surgeon.

"Do you mean to tell me we have just spent two thousand, eight hundred and thirty five pounds on new rakes that don't work?"

"It appears so."

The Chairman is clearly troubled.

Bunker rakes. Mmmmm. Puts North Korea into perspective.

At this point I feel I have to spring myself from this tourniquet trio. In my forty years in Canada I thought I had cured myself of class phobia, but clearly not.

I decide to spare them my ASDA tie and hole in the jacket. Apologising profusely and insincerely, I explain to the Chairman that because of the belated start I will not be able to socialise afterwards because I have to pick up someone (I've invented) from Canada at the station in Malton, and as we had started an hour late, I would have to leave right after the game. He pounces on the opportunity, confers with his two associates and we walk off the course on the fourteenth hole. Relief. Possibly mutual.

That very night, bank man calls me and says how much they enjoyed playing with me, and enjoyed my company (it's always what comes after the BUT that counts). But they had decided as I was, in their opinion, *living* in North Yorkshire I didn't qualify as an out of country overseas member at three hundred and forty pounds a year. However they were happy to propose me as a full member with no waiting period if I was prepared to pay three thousand, four hundred and fifty five pounds for the rest of the year. Canny businessmen. On the phone I interrupt him and terminate that idea. The conversation ends.

Weeks later I get an email from Secretary Two-Names informing me that the committee is unable to offer me Overseas Membership. I feel have been misled. It ends with the hope that I will find somewhere to play "within your golfing budget".

The rightful order of things is affirmed.

MONDAY 26TH JUNE

THE POST MISTRESS GENERAL AND THE MAGICAL MOOR

Awaking at six thirty five, but realising the loneliness and the pointlessness, I fall back into a deep, dream-filled sleep.

Get up at eleven minutes past ten.

While I do Pilates, one of the victims of a well-publicised BBC couple who enjoyed sex in public parks is being interviewed on the TV above my head. When he was fourteen, after a chance encounter in a crowded park, he was apparently groomed by a woman with a slit in her dress up to her waist, without panties. The couple were on-air hosts for the BBC.

As the victim says, "Most of my mates couldn't believe I was complaining about it. For them it would have been a dream come true. But if it was a thirty five year old man and fourteen year old girls, they would have wanted to lynch him."

The BBC couple is now doing five years in prison, for

this unorthodox, serial behaviour. I can imagine the odd Italian village celebrating this activity.

I go to the computer shop in Malton. My third-in-a-row iPod nano dies, AGAIN. Two hundred quid. Unbelievably finicky technology. The worse thing about my summer in Yorkshire is this Apple product. Can't afford another one, so ask the pock-faced nerd in the computer store what he does when he's walking down the street listening to music. I think this must be the nightmare location for a cybernerd. He knows every second away from building and demolishing intergalactic empires is wasted time, and much of that consists of giving absolutely elemental advice to uncomprehending, graying baby-boomers who come in to disturb his epic battling every fifteen minutes without fail.

"I don't deal with Apple products," he says as if I am using Grenfell Tower cladding.

He downloads MP3s from his desktop to his phone.

"Just use the cable you power it with, the android will recognise it. It has an inbuilt MP3."

"Another thing," I say, "I got a ticket from the Humberside police and they want me to copy both sides of my Canadian license and send it to them. Can I use your copier?"

He is shaking his head when I'm halfway through this request.

"Can't do that because of data corruption issues."

Oh yes. The old Data Corruption Issues. DCIs.

In times of yore, one could ask about the source cause of things and get an answer. Now the source cause of things is incomprehensible to anyone over forty five. Data Corruption Issues. Even if I understood it, would he be able to show me? Here's the distributor. See the corrosion. Thus, a short. No work. Ah, yes, I get it.

"Anywhere I can do that, as I don't have a printer?"

"Library," he offers, keen to get back to the assorted cadaverous machines (or digital victims) waiting in the back, their bellies popped open.

"Thanks."

First at the post office, I buy stamps from Attila the Huntress.

She comes across, superficially anyway, as one of the most unsympathetic public workers I have ever encountered. She stands in her own little glass booth near the door. Most people go around the corner to the two other, nicer postal clerks behind the double desk, but the queue is always twenty minutes long, and there's rarely even one person taking her on. She is quite tall in that way of powerful middle-aged women who have found their own way of countering all the crap men have thrown their way. One risks describing her as attractive, with long brown hair and challenging, prosecutorial glasses. She's probably a Brexiter with a Harley in her private life, or I don't know, a rose-gardening Anglican. This is my third visit, and she greets my questions with the raised eyebrow of a person cursed with having to deal with idiots all day long, the worst of which are foreigners. Extranjeros, uitlanders. I must be a foreigner of some kind to ask such daft questions.

"Could I have two local stamps?"

"For what?"

(For what. None of your business, ma'am.)

"An envelope. To Hull."

She sighs, long-suffering.

"Does it weigh more then twenty grams, less than twenty grams, or ten grams or below ten grams?"

(Let me just reach for that little spring scale I keep in my jacket pocket for all my crack clients at the Globe pub.)

In Canada there is one price for a local letter.

But if I am to mention this I'm risking the "well, why don't you go back to Canada" glare, I'm sure.

"I'll have two, under ten grams, local stamps please."

She tears them off like a guillotiniste.

"And two stamps overseas, Canada, under ten grams."

"Ten grams or twenty."

"Just ten."

"And do you want air mail stickers?"

"Yes, please."

She tears off one air mail sticker. One. Conversation is discouraged. She tells me the price, I pay and move aside as a small woman who looks like she is just out of bed shuffles tentatively forward to take my place before The Dark Force.

Perhaps Attila the Huntress keeps the whole town in fear.

Next stop, the library and ten pence for each copy of my Canadian license.

Then Costa, for a cappuccino and a lemon muffin and the Guardian. Theresa May is making her deal with the Ulster Protestants of Northern Ireland. The company she must keep to stay in power. It's interesting from a lesbian perspective. The only successful female Tory leader who did very well in the election was the very out head of the Scottish Conservatives. Yet May, to save her bacon, is siding with a party that bans same-sex marriages and is very anti-gay. There's always a good half hour's worth of readable material in the Guardian.

I pop next door to the fruit and veggie store. I have a strange, inexplicable craving for baked leeks covered in cheese tonight. I have never eaten this or cooked it before. It must have come to me in a dream. Or perhaps an ad subliminally absorbed. There, on display on the street, berries, tomatoes and leeks!

After a fruitless search, I ask, "You don't have mayonnaise, do you?"

"Yes, indeed I do. Locally made too."

She walks over to some unopened boxes.

"I thought it has to be refrigerated?"

"Not until you open it. It's three-pound fifty a jar."

Well. I'll try it once, I thought. Especially at that price.

A text on my cell phone. The captain of the Sheriff Hutton Second XI asking if I can umpire on Wednesday. Great. I'm a regular.

I decide to drive sixteen miles to the Moors and walk around Rosedale Abbey, a village my wife and I had stumbled into in February but had had no time to explore. On the radio on the way, on BBC 2, a Tory politician called Iain Duncan Smith is interviewing a Dutch doctor who says that dying people, in their last weeks, instead of going in for aggressive and intensive treatment, which will neither work nor give them an improved quality of life, should instead take a holiday with their loved ones. He is under attack for saying this. Mostly, of the you-never-know variety. Medical miracles. You can never dismiss one in advance!

In Rosedale Abbey, I park on the village green. A sign in a store advertises trail maps from the National Trust. Inside, a round-eyed woman is slumped against a shelf behind the cash register. Ennui radiates from her.

"Could I have one of the trail maps, please?"

"We don't have any."

"It's says you do, on the window."

"The reprinted ones haven't arrived yet."

She has that ingenuous look in her spooky eyes, like she's lying and doesn't give a shit that I know it. Strange.

"Do you know who else in the village has the maps?"

"No idea."

"Okay. Is there somebody who can tell me where I join the trail? I had it on my cell phone when I had internet access, but it's frozen here."

She sighs, and pushes herself off the shelf with the exhausted mien of a farm labourer who has been working in the fields for eighteen hours a day for eighteen years. Slip slops back into the kitchen to retrieve a second woman. She is more helpful and tells me to drive up the Bank road to a parking lot and walk along the old disused railway line that surrounds the top of the valley. It's a five and a half hour walk.

That's what I do, figuring I'll go out for one and a half hours and turn back, for three hours.

It's perfect. First I pass by the 19th century mineworks consisting of six brick arches, now filled in with time. A creature scurries across a hillock below me.

It stops and turns its head to clock me, frozen. Brown fur, cream neck and under-fur. Beautiful. Nat Geo. I reach for my camera-phone but the animal dips into a hole and is gone. The whole hillock is riddled with holes. At night it must be like King's Cross for critters.

"Hey man. What's shakin'?" (I see a cartoon series.)

"Whatcha git today, man?" Pencil-moustached Weasel with silver-banded tooth-pick.

"A vole, a mole and two mice, man."

I'm wondering if they all come out at night, like Montrealers onto their balconies, to chew the fat.

Later I look him up. It's a stoat. I thought stoats were

a blur. This fella was as still as a painting, handsome and proud.

The Moors are deceptive. It resembles a still life. Potential for spookiness. But beneath the stillness, a thousand hearts beat, water and sap flows in a hundred ways, petals blink at you from unexpected nooks, like stars. There are sheep everywhere. Grouse-like birds erupt under one's feet, flapping furiously. No wonder they are such easy prey for shooters. They wait until you are right on top of them, then making the maximum racket, they fly clumsily a few feet above the ground at shoulder height. Lift, bang, dog, fetch. Lift, bang, dog, fetch. Lift, bang, whoops, Cheney. They appear to nest snuggled into the base of bushes. I roll my fist into one freshly abandoned nest and I fancy I can still feel the warmth of the bird's body. If only they knew my intentions, they could have stayed where they were.

A shrieking bird with a curly feather sticking up from her head flies towards my head and circles back, seemingly terrified that I am going to find whatever she flew away from, presumably her chicks. Later I look it up. It's the Northern Lapwing.

Another long-beaked bird coasts by, pealing. Later I see that it may be a Eurasian Curlew.

The fields are different shades of green along the entire valley. But closer, there is a profusion of colours hidden in the brown-grey moor around me. Isolated stalks of prickly heather, scrub, bush, gorse, purple florets, and outbursts of white flowers, which on closer inspection reveal cotton headed blossoms, as if the sheep have left a hundred little bits of themselves on tiny stems strong enough to withstand the constant winds.

The ground itself is springy, and every shade of black and brown and in one stretch, chalky. Sometimes it gives in to my footfall, other times it crunches as if scorched, at others it is as hard as a sunbaked cricket pitch.

Beneath my well-shod feet, there's every variation of vegetation, but subtle, almost camouflaged. Virgin's moss, lichen-like cavemen's paintings, tussocks of turf, marsh, fen, fern, whisp reed and chokers' sand.

As I walk along I practice my umpiring "OUT" signal. It's a finger up in the air. I do the erect, high imperial one. No, definitely not. Number two, a sort of wheeling motion ending in the finger up. No!

Number three, a drumroll, like Keith Moon might do it. Spinning the drumstick and ending either in OUT or NOT OUT.

I settle for a head lowered, arm out to the side, finger raised no higher than the shoulder, one. That'll be mine. Gentle, unflappable and firm at the same time. The face slightly down, as if regretful, every dismissal like a small bird hitting a cliff. It's only village cricket, in a cricketing paradise. Few are aware of heaven. They're too busy handling all the shit that's coming at them every day. Bills, heartaches, the boss. Some of the village players look like they've had their donnybrooks, but elsewhere, at rugby league or the pub or footie, but not at cricket.

The wind is really affectionate today. I feel it's stroking my neck and head.

I turn onto a path away from the valley and in ten minutes reach a road, single lane from left to right, cars whizzing by. Where Man Intrudes. Steel and rubber, the whine. Every ten paces there's a piece of junk, plastic, a can of bitter, or cider, a plastic coke or sprite or energy drink, plastic bags, discarded tissues.

I dream up a reality TV show 'The Litterers'. Put up cameras on a stretch like this for two months. Get an audience to vote on what the appropriate punishment should be for those who litter and are caught by their license plates. Camera crews and hairpiece hosts will track the car to a home, and do the trivial doorstep prosecution, a thousand dartpricks of rage falling down upon the transgressor's head. Depending on the culprit. If it's a kid, get him or her to spend an hour cleaning up fifty yards in a driving rainstorm.

"Clive. Spell C_L_I_M_A_T_E CHANGE."

I spot the outline of a sheep carcass behind a bush. I go over to it. It's like installation art. Was it hit and removed to this spot, behind the first bush? Was it hit and wobbled over here to die? Or did it just die here of old age? Or of Moors Sheep disease. Bones are pushing through the lifeless fleece to the sky, flies and carrion birds having their go. On the road, roadkill. Pheasants mostly, a few quail. The cars whoosh by. Sheep graze on the very edge. A ewe lies with two lambs in a nest of purple brush.

Here's another idea: a series of double page photographs in the Guardian. A picture like the one I have just taken of mamma sheep and her twin lambs in the purple heather. That picture with the caption 'May strikes deal with DUP'. 'PM denies leadership revolt.' Or 'US manufacturer withdraws Grenfell cladding'. The indifference of nature to the big daily news.

Suddenly there's a pond with perfect reeds, a few sunken feet from the hissing tyres. There were potholes earlier. This is a place where things are hidden.

There's a mirage over the hill ahead which turns into the chrome reflection of a car parked at right angles to the road, just off to one side. It's a black Hyundai, and as I walk, I observe several key chains between the seats. "You can tell a lot about a man from his keys and his shoes," someone once said. Me, probably.

As I crest the small hill leading back to the valley, I pass a strange three-walled open structure with the words Falkirk 3 on a plaque.

The wind is up a bit and there's a little nip. As I put on my sleeveless sweater, a couple with a black lab are coming towards me. If it's their car, black is clearly their colour. Dog, car, clothing. The woman is wearing black leather.

"I wonder what that is?" I say, gesturing to the open structure.

"There's a couple more back there," he says. "There's

sheep droppings in them. But I found some cartridges on the outside."

"Ahh." I draw my walking stick up like aiming a rifle.

"They must be blinds."

The couple have more studs on them than an S and M bedhead.

He is burly, short haired, barrel-chested, well-muscled, about forty with a stud in his earlobe and his right nostril. That one seems to be screwed through his septum. She has dyed short red-hair and studs in her ears, mouth, nose, and who knows where else.

They have strong accents.

I imagine a conversation with them.

"May I ask you a personal question?"

"Why not?"

"Are you two into kinky sex?"

"Well. That is quite the question." He smiles. "Yes we are, as a matter of fact."

"I could tell by the studs. The ones I could see, anyway."

"Are you?"

"Me! What?"

"Into kinky sex."

"No-no. I am the Anti-Climax."

He bursts into laughter.

I move off.

"Have yourself a fine day."

"You too," he shouts.

A rampant sheep, the biggest one I have seen, canters across the path just ahead. Stops. Looks around. Peers at me momentarily, then canters off again, at real speed. The King Sheep. Or Ram. I've never seen a sheep that large move that urgently. Soon after I see a lamb ramming its face into its mamma's teats. But then as I pass closer, the mamma has horns. Do ewes have horns? What is going on? The moors. A blank canvas with all sorts of magic going on.

I re-find the old railway line path and turn back. Now that I have no audiobooks, no working iPod, I have to kill the hours it will take me to get back. I stop.

It's that moment that occurs every walk. Stop, look, look around you, Nature. Stop. Stop time. Stop life. Stop the continuum of your life. This is Blake's speck of dust. Right here. Everywhere. I look around.

Above me there is a layer of clouds as far as the eye can see, clouds with dark undersides, holding rain but not yet giving it up. My eyes follow the clouds, into its curves and clefts, the gap between them which never finds clear air but folds into the next cloud and the next and on and on. I follow the clouds from left to right looking up at an angle of about fifteen degrees and my eyes sweep across and above the end of the valley and around to the other side.

The line of hills beyond is very very gentle and clear as can be, no mountains, peaks or other interruptions. The line is smooth and wavers only very slightly. I feel the crunch of roots beneath my feet as I stand there almost still, except for the slow turn as I follow the line of the hillsides beyond, on the other side of the valley. I sense that World War One soldiers in the muddy death fields of France, working men from the Yorkshire Moors must have evoked this visual memory in a crisis, and other Yorkshire wanderers, squeezed out from any hope of ownership and security by hierarchy and inherited property, must have gone to the far flung corners of the earth in times when it was impossible to return, to buy a ticket and fly back, and hold this sight in their hearts and souls again. On the far side I spot four lumps on the hill line. I have no idea what they are. I hear an imaginary local say, "Oh, it's just the buildings on High Farm, The Hutton place," or whatever. I finally reach the end of my circumscan and let my eyes fall down into the valley, deeper than the fields of sheep and all the hedges and walls that may have been there for decades upon decades. I can't even see Rosedale Abbey, where tea awaits. I finally let go and break the spell of the circle. I start to walk back along the covered old railway line, where iron mined by hand was doubtless put on rattling cars and hauled someplace like Middlesbrough, the port over the Moors to the north. I pass a stone and wood bench with an inscription: '*In the dark, working hard, loading up the wooden cart*'.

Two hours to go. So I start to try to remember the boys on my school rugby team.

It wasn't a very good team, I remember, sure we didn't

have a winning record. In my last year I was captain. I got over this, decades ago.

Front row.

'Bobo' Olsen, Benger, Mike Slutzkin

Back Row

Bonny Ballantyne, McKay, Currie

#8 Mad Mike Kenny

Halves:

Julian Caldow and Derek Morphew (Morphew became a very prominent evangelist)

Backs:

Key, Dallamore, Heaton-Nicholls, Barrell

Fullback

Kisch

I remember their faces, scraps of memory. Slowing it down to make the time pass with every step towards home now. It takes me through a fair stretch.

Then I count to eight hundred, pushing my pace, finishing the last of my water.

At three minutes past four, I get back to the parking lot, fold myself into the car, and lean back, closing my eyes, savouring the relief, the end. I descend to the same cafe, buy cheese for the roasted leeks and a cup of tea.

"Did you have a good walk?" the friendly lady asks.

"Magnificent."

Outside I noticed the sign. For sale.

"Is this the place for sale?" I ask.

"Yes." She puts up her left hand like a clever pupil. "It's mine."

"How long have you owned it?"

She thinks.

"Fif-teen years." She is tired.

"Hard work, huh?"

"Very. Especially when you have to do all the baking."

"I knew some people in Toronto who owned restaurants and it was very tiring. And they didn't do the baking."

I pay for my stuff, adding a bottle of shandy for when I get home, for the writing.

"What are you doing tomorrow?" she asks.

"I thought I'd take my wife to see the David Hockney museum."

"That's in West Yorkshire."

"I know."

When I get back, the leeks and cheese are amazing.

WEDNESDAY 28TH JUNE

THE ANGRY BOWLER

No place as great as this can stay peaceful and harmonious forever.

I am texted to umpire the Sheriff Hutton 2nd X1 home game, about ten minutes' drive away. The visiting team, Boston Spa, looks a little serious, stationary-jogging on the green. Marion, our gravel-voiced scorer growls that we will lose, because our opening batsman and opening bowlers have both been stolen by the 1st X1, and the Boston Spa team should be in the first division anyway. Out in the middle, part of my job is to put the stumps in. But the ground is so hard and the holes so small I can't get them all the way in. This means the stumps will stand higher than they should, creating the possibility of false outs. A member of the visiting team suggests I soften the holes by pouring a bit of water into them. I do and wait a few minutes as the teams take the field. I place a stump back, borrow a bat and thump the top of the stump with the handle end of the bat. A spray of mud splatters onto my white coat, and into my face. Serves me right. My umpire's white coat is now in character, mud-spotted. It's a sign.

During the match I get a waft of something different. Aggro.

The visitors bat first and are about 90 for 5 when a handsome, bearded young left-hander comes to wicket, takes some massive swishes and declares that he hasn't played for five years.

Another massive swish and I am thinking if he connects I'll have to introduce the back-up ball, as the game ball will be well and truly gone into yonder cornfield between the big Oak and the castle with its teetering corner.

He does connect and blisters his way to a fifty with five sixes.

The ball begins to whine off his bat like a mortar. I don't quite believe he hasn't batted for five years, partly on account of his beautiful gear and expensive bat well bruised with red welts. His partner informs me he is a very good hockey player, the field variety, which explains his eye.

Come Sheriff Hutton's innings and he opens the bowling, spraying fast in-swinging left arm deliveries left and right.

"I haven't bowled for five years," he confides on his way past me, back to his mark.

But one ball an over is terrific. In the fourth over a ball drifts in late onto the stumps but seams wickedly away, thwacking the batsman on his front-foot pad very much in front. Very Wasim Akram. There is a furious appeal, our hero all spittle and certainty. I am reminded of Mel Gibson in Braveheart.

"NOT OUT," I proclaim, and look down at the stones my wife has reikied and which I use to count the six balls of each over. Four left.

I hear spikes crunching towards me and feel his breath on my cheek. It's vaguely redolent of rotting swamp frogs.

"Slidin' Down?" A query between clenched teeth, meaning is the delivery sliding down legside.

I am monkish. Saying nothing.

"SLIDIN' DOWN?"

Bearded Warrior is breathing on me, an inch or two from my face. Like an Afrikaans Interrogator in the Bad Old Days.

Silence.

Then, sotto voce, I murmur, "Not out."

Hrrrmph, a little speckle of his sweat, or spit hits my cheek as he stomps off. Less than a spit, but in the same insult spectrum.

Later I thought I should have asked him if he'd ever seen Kill Bill.

And he would've said, "Ma favourite movie."

I also thought I should face him, give him a look that I am not to be trifled with or intimidated. Or just turn into Werewolf Ump and claw his face off his skull right there and then and fold it into my white pocket with the reikied stones.

I think about this later. Umpiring must be the absence

of all ego, or bad temper. And this is a status devoutly to be wished. For me, a curative. Ever since the age of ten when Miss Spicer, the judge, told me, "One day I'll see you at the Old Vic," after giving me the gold medal for my recitation of four verses of The Rime of The Ancient Mariner at the Emmarentia Eisteddfod of 1961, I am somewhat afflicted by a towering and insatiable ego. An ego which feeds on excessive praise. The Golden Caress. The Honeyed Lick. Finally in 2017, in North Yorkshire, umpiring, I have found its antidote. The absence of ego. For with ego, a position of authority becomes a red rag to all the bulls. Both the young blue-eyed, red-bearded bulls, and the old, shrivelled, canny, back-bent-by-fortune bulls. But if one lacks ego, one is impervious to goading. And one is not provocative. The facts are the facts. The ball, in fact, in my opinion, while being a very good delivery, is *possibly* seaming past the offstump, giving the batsman that wonderful thing called the "benefit of the doubt".

This comes to me many weeks later, in fact, on a Monday morning after I see the fourth day of the third test from the Oval. Aleem Dar, who I have seen preside over many tests all over the world, has another excellent day behind the stumps, making several critical decisions that are extremely close, but exactly correct, as the slow-motion replay proves. A feathered nick onto the pads comes mind. One of the bowlers, Stuart Broad, I think it is, a slightly histrionic performer, is giving Dar that you-ran-over-my-dachshund look, but Dar is impervious, a servant to the facts, as only he is authorised to determine. Everyone else has an interest, a bias. And yes, the thought does occur to me that in this day and age of Islamic extremism, Dar's imperturbable and uninfluenceable calm could be useful. Though he could be a Christian, a Hindu, a theosophist, for all I know.

If he is from Pakistan, remember this. The photograph in my World Press Photo book for 2017 of Pakistani lawyers lying dead and wounded on the ground after a mass bombing. In their suits, white shirts bloodied, some frozen in friezes of anguish and severe pain. While this might be a step too far, the neutral arbiter of justice in the frontlines of extremism is a man or woman to be profoundly valued.

In the end, Sheriff Hutton loses convincingly. I imagine one day they will turn to me, and I shall bat them to victory. Down, ego, down.

FRIDAY 7TH JULY
THRUMS AND LORD'S

Finally my weekend in London is here!

Last night, in the caravan, there is a tremendous deluge. Big black clouds build up north of the park, and for half an hour unload like cats and dogs. Water courses between the caravans, instant streams. The roof thrums like it is being pounded by a police water cannon.

We watch some TV and Nicky goes to bed. I pack for London and step out onto the deck for a smoke. The moon is fringing a post storm wispy cloud. It's velvet, after the tempest.

In the morning, Nicky drops me at the station in good time. I ask the ticket officer for confirmation of my departure, the eleven-thirteen to York, then ask him where the toilets are.

"Across the road. At boess stayshun."

A woman behind me in a striking floral dress adds, "…despite years of requests for ones here in the station, sorry to say," as if delivering an official apology from the people of Malton to me, the outsider.

I balance my overloaded knapsack, Guardian and cappuccino out of the station, past the Jobs plus Centre, over the busy road to a blue door at the bus station. It demands ten pence in a slot next to the Gents door. I fumble, squirming my one free hand past cell-phone, sweetener dispenser, lighter, cig pack, pound notes into the depths of my pocket to extricate my coins, past all the same obstacles, all while holding coffee, newspaper and knapsack in left hand. I drop the knapsack. The only coins I have are pounds and fifty pences. In goes the fifty. First door open but a second one jams. I eventually put my shoulder into it and it explodes inwards, clanking off the wall and nearly levelling me on the rebound. I have twenty minutes until the train. A third door to the lavatory itself also sticks. I take a breath and shiver with annoyance. Then I think. If this is the only thing that stresses you in your new life, it ain't much. I pop the door with my shoulder and the lid of my awful railway café cappuccino pops off and the coffee cascades to the floor, Fortunately it pools in such a way that I can hop over it to get to the loo. I slam the door to. I sit down. Soon I hear the first, outer door pop, then the second inner door crashes open.

Someone is in the toilet with me. I am reading the Guardian, the coverage of Joe Root's magnificent 180 not out at Lord's yesterday. That's where I'm heading. Lord's.

"Hello," I hear.

"Yes?" I reply.

"You alright?"

"Yes, fine thank you."

"I saw the spilled coffee and thought maybe you had collapsed in there."

A clue in a noir scene. I saw the coffee spilled violently on the floor, officer. The door swung open to my touch. An older man lay there crumpled on the floor, his pants down, blood seeping into the coffee, his Guardian stained red and brown.

"No. I dropped the coffee. I'm fine."

"Righty then."

"Do you want to use this?" I ask.

"No-no. I'm off."

I hear the tap run, and the door close, and after he leaves, I murmur, "Thanks for asking."

What an end that would be, I thought. B Taplow Bucks April 15th 1951, d Malton bus station gents toilet, July 7th 2017.

Some would say, very appropriate. "He was a first class bullshitter," said Edward Fassley-Willard, an ex-schoolfriend.

I wonder if the stranger will report me to the Malton Bus Station maintenance man.

"'There's a man in there, 'as spilled 'is coffee everywhere. Bet 'e won't clean it oopp."

" 'E bloody well will now." Reaching for his cosh, wiping 'is bacon butty crumbs from his moufe.

In the loo, I fold up my Guardian, thinking, I better get

the hell out of here. I reach under the white plastic paper dispenser but there's nothing there. I mean there are rolls there, I can see two of them through the little perspex window. But neither is dangling down that critical bit to pull. I put my hand under the one that I can reach and feel for the end piece, but nothing. I think I can hear Biff the Cleaner's knuckles dragging along the asphalt outside as he makes his way to confront the coffee-spiller. I spin the roll with increasing intensity. I check the time. Ten minutes to departure. Still no purchase. I dig my nails into the side of the roll, twisting my left wrist. Don't want to shorten my golf season with a Malton Bus Station loo paper dispenser left wrist strain.

I can hear Dr Longwood, the nice NHS doctor I had seen, saying, his head shaking sadly, "Well what we have here is a macillus metacarpal sheath extensor strain… you'll need three months rehab… percocets…"

I hear the outer door creak open.

Merde!

I tear at the roll, and it eventually yields a lump of papers, I tear it off unevenly until a pile of ravaged loo paper lies at my feet which I of course slide over to absorb the spilled coffee.

The inner door opens with protest and a bang as it too bounces off the wall. I freeze, except for my left foot which sidefoots the rest of the torn paper over the coffee.

Is that heavy breathing? A grunt. The man is relieving himself.

Phew.

He leaves, I stand, pull my trousers on, and get out of there.

I half expect to see a truckload of pigs spilled open between me and the station. I wonder what Rowan Atkinson would have done with the Malton Bus Station Loo Disaster. I have left a coffee mess for the cleaner, and silently apologise. He's probably got the right tools to clean it in a jiffy. It must be said it was a very clean loo, smelling of antiseptic, when I got there.

The York-bound train pulls into the lovely small station at Malton, with its flowerpots between the benches and its decorated trellis posts supporting the roof above the passenger platform. On the train, there's not a seat to be found. I stand in the passageway between two cars. Soon after we leave there's an announcement.

"If there is anybody on board who can deal with a medical emergency, would they please make their way to the middle of coach D."

That's me. Us. Sure enough, halfway up the car there's a knot of conductors, and two women, one from the front and one from the rear, two seats in front of me, make their way to the ailing one.

The countryside flying past is beautifully green, with little storybook farms, and sheepies and cowies spotting the meadows. The women look like nurses and remind me of World War Two and underground bomb shelters.

As one of the conductors walks by me with his walkie-talkie, I say, "May I ask you a question?"

"Yes?"

"Why do you sell tickets if you don't have seats?"

"Because the ticket only guarantees you passage, not seats."

"Oh."

A dainty little bespectacled lady below me turns and offers her seat.

"No, no, no. I'm fine." Then loudly, in my Canadian accent I say, in a friendly enough manner, "It's just that in Canada when they sell you a ticket it comes with a seat." I have no idea if that's true, but I am enjoying the dynamic.

I know, I know, there are more important things happening with the chap (assume it's a chap) in mortal danger (though it seems lighter than that). I just like to be a selfish prick sometimes. It's a symptom of my happiness.

Let me digress. There are rabbits in the caravan park where I now live. They are responsible, I am told, for the ten little holes in our lawn. I dutifully transfer dirt from the flowerbed and fill up the holes, spreading three pounds worth of grass seed on the replacement dirt. Next morning I come out, *and the holes are back.*

I ask one of the golfers who's been talking about gardening about this.

"Waste of time," he says. "Rabbits will be back and do it again and again."

"Why?" I say, repressing thoughts of extermination.

"They just like to toss things around, throw things about."

I can relate to this. In South Africa we used to call it shit-disturbing. In fact, Nelson Mandela's middle name, the name he is given at birth, is Rolihlahla, a Xhosa word meaning he who shakes the tree. Why does he shake the tree? Why? Why? Why?

And if you are a tree-shaker and cause problems for others, your own tree will, in turn, be shaken. The rabbits will dig their holes in your own lawn.

I get to York in good time, and on the platform I pass a stretcher full of emergency workers, laughing about something, waiting for the stricken passenger. I imagine the man (if it is a man) is having an attack of unhappiness, and all he wants is some attention, and these laughing lasses are hired by the state to give him a little tenderness.

I get another cuppa and a chicken something at Starbucks, and make the train to King's Cross in time. I have an assigned seat # 26 in coach D. The train is close to full, but the window seat #25 is unoccupied when we pull out one minute late at four minutes past twelve. I slide across immediately and claim it. Although we have had four stops, so far, I am still in the window seat, with mine still empty to my left.

And South Africa bowls England out for 458. Although I only have tickets for the Sunday, I might pop down there this aft!

Lovely stuff.

Across from me a wrinkled woman with a sunken eye and hair all dun up luvly savours a ripe black plump cherry. I mean, savours it. Rolls it around in her mouth and then bites into it. She may be blind, or partially blind. They say all the others senses are enhanced.

She boarded at Doncaster. Off to London. It'll be a scorcher.

SUNDAY 9TH JULY

DEBACLE AT LORD'S

SA get hammered by England at Lord's. It is a pretty abject performance, one of their worst since readmission.

I am a little slow getting going and only make it to the ground at noon. South Africa has ripped through the English middle order, Morkel, Rabada and Maharaj doing the damage. All out, leaving SA 320 to win.

Lord's is a great spectacle, fifty thousand, mostly male middle class and up, overwhelmingly white. Lots of South Africans. Many more beet-faced Englishmen. At one corner of the ground there's a garden, the Harris Garden, a drinking garden it seems, populated by men wearing the startling yellow and red colours of the Marylebone Cricket Club, and women in colourful dresses and floppy hats. They seem less interested in cricket than getting pole-axed drunk. It gets louder and louder in there.

Inside the stadium, a single wren darts back and forth on the baize-like outfield, pecking away at the grass.

South Africa needs a heroic innings from someone,

but they fold against Ali's unremarkable off-spin. South Africans have never been able to play spin bowling. The pitch is a bit dusty, with the odd ball kicking sideways, but nobody seems to put their heart into it. JP Duminy hits a lovely shot right into midwicket's hands, and as he trudges off one has the feeling one may never see him play cricket for South Africa again. Apart from two or three epic innings he never fulfilled his potential.

I bump into Mike Procter, the great all rounder, who I had played against at school in Natal. He remembers my team but not the details. When I tell him the name of my school, he turns away, pretending to spurn me, but spins back with a big grin on his face. He now runs a training academy at Ottawa Primary School in Durban, for disadvantaged black children. It doesn't look great from the website, but I shall read more about it in his book, which I buy, and enjoy. If I had been a professional cricketer I may have lived a life close to his, though I was nowhere near as talented. In fact, let me correct that. If I had been a professional cricketer it would have been an unrewarding grind. But I will never know. At the time I felt I could, and wanted to, play any bowler in the world, especially the great West Indians.

Because the match ends early with an England win, I walk to King's Cross to catch the train back to Yorkshire. My revulsion at South Africa's lame capitulation subsides on the stroll. It takes me across Regent's Park, where my mother walked me as a baby. She told me the Queen drove by one day, and she lifted my hand from the pram, and the Queen waved back. We used to mimic that famous wave, and laugh about it. On the large meadow, about five cricket matches are underway. Couples cuddling in the grass, as ever. Beyond the Park I get a bit lost in the dead end streets of Regents Park housing estate but eventually find King's Cross in time for a salad at Pret-a-Manger.

Now flying along the rails, the setting sun strobes though the towers as we head north.

WEDNESDAY 12TH JULY

THE SAD GOLFER

This morning two of my playing partners are Geoff and Ted. Geoff is a terse, wristy player who is very accurate and had once been a five handicap. It transpires he too is going to Royal Birkdale for the Open on Sunday July 23rd. He suggests I download The App. Ted is a lefty who takes no time at all, no practice swing, down the middle almost every time, and a former President of the Club. Our third player hardly says a thing the whole round. There's an aura of sadness around him.

On the 18th, Geoff explains.

"He lost his wife last year. They had just moved into a new house together."

In the parking lot, the sad golfer and I find ourselves walking together to the bar. He had told me in our only on-course conversation that he followed the cricket closely. I ask him if he had played himself.

"Yes, until the age of thirty. In the Yorkshire senior league."

I know this means he had to be pretty good.

"What did you do?" I ask.

"Opening batsman."

"So was I."

"But I had four daughters to raise so I stopped."

When we go to the bar, he sits opposite me and I notice he has blue eyes. But his face is a mask of sadness.

I feel comforted that he has four daughters. I have only one and she is a joy. I find myself refraining from asking him about them, and grandchildren, in case tragedy lies there too.

I have escaped this kind of deep, unassuageable pain in my own life. I fear when I see it in others. My sister lost a son. There is no relief from this. Ever.

I stay awhile, having a lager shandy and a chicken coronation on toasted brown.

On the way back, in Malton, I stop to pick up the jacket that had its hole in the front of the pocket mended.

Once home, I nap, and at five fifteen wake to prepare for the cricket game at home against Rowntrees and Huntington.

"They beat us last time. Youngsters," says the old off-spin bowler.

The young off-spin bowler is crotchety and cynical. He doesn't strike me as a happy young man.

Sheriff Hutton manage to dismiss the young team for 72, and are doing quite well chasing when the captain runs out of batsmen. The grumpy offspinner, the second last decent batsman, gets a ball above his head from a slow bowler and flails at it tennis-style into the air and is caught at cover. He is waving his arms at me demanding a no-ball. Late, and believing a no-ball to be above the waist, I signal no ball and he is not out. The fielding side protests. The bowler says spinners have to bowl the bowl above the shoulder for it to be deemed a no ball. I may have been slow off the mark, but the ball is above the shoulder and therefore it's the right decision. But by not knowing the shoulder rule, I had caused some confusion.

Rowntrees has a very, very good fielder who takes the other threatening batsman low down at long-on, a tumbling catch, finely judged. Then he throws down the stumps from midwicket on the other side with a rocket. The visitors have drive and enthusiasm whereas Sheriff's exhibit a certain lack of confidence. Momentum in cricket. When you have seen as much of this glorious, intricate game as I have, it's often over before it's over. Wickets *tumble.*

I have to turn down some lbw asks with a bowler who is angling quick deliveries down the leg-side.

Rowntrees prevail when the number eleven batsman, the aforementioned old offspinner, faces the last ball needing six to win and cues it harmlessly up to silly mid wicket for the final out. From the celebration by the visitors, I gather extra points are accrued for an outright win, removing all ten batsmen.

Sheriff allows one to slip away.

Tomorrow to Oxford. Long drive. To see a play.

FRIDAY 14TH JULY

A GREAT PERFORMANCE

Last night saw Nicky's friend Nick Woodeson as Willy Loman in Death of a Salesman at the Oxford Playhouse. Wrenching performance by Nick, a small, intense, mannered actor who is highly effective in the role. Such a depressing but powerful play, dated and relevant at the same time. The rest of the cast is uneven, the set one of the worst I've seen. Devoid of a great opportunity for period detail, the fifties in New York. A big empty space with the words THE LAND OF THE FREE emblazoned across the back wall. That's it. Over-stating the obvious, one thinks.

Interestingly, I read in the programme notes that the FBI tried to ban the play from being shown because of its negative depiction of American values.

We walk around Oxford a bit. The height of tourist season almost subsumes the dreaming spires, but you can see behind the noisy clumps of foreign visitors and language students just enough of the manicured quadrangles, ancient sandstone and windowed studies.

The drive back from Oxford is a trial. More than five hours, whereas the drive down there takes three and a half. It is a Friday, joining northwards traffic from London.

I manage to bring in the radio commentary of the second test, day one from Trent Bridge.

The reason we have to drive back is so I can make a talk by the golf caddie Billy Foster at the Scarborough club.

After the debacle with Ganton, I am determined to dress properly and bring an excellent blue tie with yellow flowers and the repaired jacket.

I walk into the dining area. Foster is already speaking to a full house of members and not one of them is wearing either a tie or a jacket. Got it wrong, again. I find a seat at the back next to the bar, and try to get a lager shandy but the bartender points admonishingly at his watch as if I missed inspection or something, before leaning forward and taking my whispered request.

Foster stands at the other side of the room, his back to the door windows looking out over the first hole and the sea beyond. He is a local lad from Keighley in Yorkshire and proceeds to tell a series of great yarns about some of the best players in the world for whom he caddied over a PGA career of seventeen years.

The best of these stories could be titled, 'The Greatest Shot ever Played." It is Switzerland 1993, the European Masters. On the final day, Seve Ballesteros birdies five holes in a row to tie for the lead. But he pulls his tee shot over a wall and some trees. Caddy Billy strongly believes Seve should chip it out, behind him to safety.

"I have thees shot," Seve says. "Chew don't unnerstand my game."

Billy insists.

Seve demands, "How far am I from the green?"

Billy pops his head out from the wall and the trees and says 140. Not really measuring it, just guessing, no heart in it. He hands him a chipper. Seve is peering at the trees beyond the wall. Billy sees he is eyeing a hole in the tree about the size of a dinner plate. Seve grabs a pitching wedge, couches down low to the ball, flails with all his might. The ball clears the wall by a fraction, pierces the dinner plate, ends up just short of the green. Seve chips in for the birdie and the trophy.

Foster then grabs his glass, raises it, looks up and says, "Here's to the Greatest Golfer Who Ever Played", and everyone does likewise, toasting Seve The Great.

MONDAY 17TH JULY

LOST IN LEVISHAM

It seems I have been knocked off my routine a bit. Today, I resolve to walk and write once again.

Pretty well at random I choose a second walk from Paddy Dillon's Walking the North York Moors.

Number 5: Levisham Station, Levisham and Newtown-on-Rawcliffe.

We never make it to Newtown-on-Rawcliffe, but more on that later.

The road penetrates the Moors past Pickering, climbs and forks between two banks. Around the first corner an "Oh Robin" view of the thick green valley opens up. (These moments of unalloyed joy greet one on every excursion and invigorate a relationship like ours. Thirty four years married. We are so privileged to be together, healthy, and be, unexpectedly, in this glorious place. Something to pause on, to value, and give thanks for.)

In fact, let me pause here and talk about my wife Nicky. I love her so much. She is so different from me. A sceptical

North American, a restless intelligence, a woman of great acting talent who, just two weeks ago travelled to London to perform her one-woman show at her alma mater, the Royal Academy of Dramatic Art. Having not done "Hooked" for a year. People who went were blown away. Also she's the mother of our three children. Tenacious and deeply loving. Both details and grand themes are handled with great commitment.

Back to walk #5. Through Lockton and Levisham and the road narrows even more. At one point, a truck's descending grille looms in our windscreen but everyone is on the correct line so we swoosh by, by a coat of paint.

Speaking of a coat of paint, often used to invoke the margin by which a fast cricket ball misses a stump, I had left the desperate English cricket team to their miserable fate at the hands of the South Africans at Trent Bridge. Needing 474 to win, and two days to do it, facing Morkel, Philander, Morris, Olivier and Maharaj, and the wily captaincy of Francois du Plessis, there is no serious talk of them succeeding. Du Plessis has to be in SA for the birth of his first child during the Lord's defeat. Graeme Smith describes him as the best looking South African test captain ever. He's known as Faff, no doubt from what are described as Afrikaner roots, but I like to give the Huguenots credit. They brought Labuschagnes, Du Toits and De Villiers to South Africa. Du Plessis has the flashing eyes and physical poise, if not natural swagger, of a swashbuckler from the Napoleonic Age.

I had resolved not to hear the score as I am taping the day's play.

After fringing the prettiest valley, we drop down to Levisham Station, which is just that, and very little else. A tiny toy station on a steam train line between Pickering and the sea, some eighteen miles long.

I had managed to get lost using the Moors book on a previous walk, walk #1, East Ayton, so I asked Nicky, slightly better at details, to navigate. We rise gently through woods, and up to the most sweetly cut grass path angling up to the ridge. Even though the ridge circling the valley seems so high, the walk is comparatively gentle. We talk. I hug her at one point. I make a note to remember the conversation as it flows so smoothly between us, but now it escapes me. At the top we look down on a valley divided into various colours. I say, "Look at that."

The green of the woods, that field with the purple hazy grasses, the river bushes, the fields beyond with dark hedges. She says, "The brown fields."

"They look purple to me."

"It's not a criticism," she says.

And we are cross at each other for a few hundred yards. Things can flip between us in a nanosecond. Bliss to clash.

After forty minutes, we follow the book to the village of Levisham, which looks like an entrant in the Yorkshire Village of the Year competition, or a film set.

We take some pictures and follow the road sharply downhill, zig-zagging until we see a footpath sign on the left which has the words Tabular Hills on it. It seems steep and overgrown but we follow it to a medieval church, abandoned with a plaque, which has pictures of the 10th and 12th century relics.

Who dies here?
What dies here?
Stones are so ancient
There are two recent graves, though
2005
2009
Women
Why?
Did they want to be buried near their forebears?

The church itself is roofless
Open to the skies
And birds and bats
The floor reeks,
Behind a fence at the altar
Ancient icons
Crosses
Lay in broken pieces.

Beyond the church
It says
A footbridge crosses a river
As do we
And pause to admire
The babbling brook

And move again
Through gate and path
Towards a waterfall sound
Through the trees
We stand above it
Looking at each other
In the insect-humming glade
And I say
"Ten Years Married
We'd have our clothes off
And into there."
We would fall
To beat the heat
But now
We see danger
In the slippery green slime
The water rushes down.

We walk on and stop
The Pause that inhales
The sounds
Birdsong
The wind
Breeze bending grasses
The layers of green to the ridge above
The light blue sky
Cloudless
Circling our heads
Taking it ALL in.

Moments like this
Become eternal
And are like Death
At its best
Its very best.

We walk on through gates past a raggedy small herd, and Nicky stands right on a big fresh patty. We press on into a wood where the road, despite the heat, becomes perilously muddy, and the book says beneath us to the right is a marsh conservation area fed by alkaline waters, and into a clear field where pheasant erupt and alight halfway up and trot across a road path.

In our reverie, we lose our way.

Pheasant path is the one we should have taken but didn't, getting lost in the wood road with mud until we reach the railway line again and at one farm, not even a village, Farwal, with the promised tea garden, empty and abandoned.

We decide to follow the railway line.
I CHOOSE THE WRONG DIRECTION
OH YES I DO
and we walk for an hour stopping to eat half a Lindt salted caramel chocolate bar
and slug water where the rail-line crosses a stream
which I should have used to *fill* the water bottle
but we walk on and on and on,
at one point it feels like

Lost in the Transvaal
On some backwoods
Dirt track
Sun beating down
Too tired to look out for snakes
In a clear-cut forestry plantation
Nicky's hat exhaustedly angled
Hands on hips
Keeping distance
Plodding on.
Then in a clearing I check my cell phone bearings
and we are in
THE MIDDLE OF NOWHERE.

Our only escape seems to be crossing the railway and the river and climbing a wild ridge to a road I see on the GPS map. Which we do and exhausted and out of water, we phone the Pickering Taxi and are picked up eventually by a lovely woman cabbie at Mudd's farm on the Whitby road. She gasps with joy when she takes us back through the lovely hidden views of Levisham. Which she has never seen before. A one-a-half hour walk turns into almost five. Lost and found.

And SA bowls out England for 130-odd, winning the Second Test and tie-ing the series. Why it's four tests, instead of five, escapes me.

Back home, I buy a beer and Sprite and fast-forward through the wicket carnage before passing out alongside

Nicky who held up well on our meandering trek, very plucky.

TUESDAY 18TH JULY

THE SALTAIRE VISIONARY

Cachuck, cachuk whizzing by
Riding
The ribbon of death.

Down the juddering motorway, to Saltaire today, an entire factory and housing complex near Leeds built by the industrialist Sir Titus Salt in 1853. Massive settlement, brought back to life after bankruptcy of the textile company in the 1980s by a visionary entrepreneur, the late Jonathon Silver. David Hockney described him as the one person, outside his own family, that he is closest to in the UK and Hockney is central to what Silver creates there.

In the modernised factory, a huge and wonderful room about two hundred feet long displays Hockney prints, sketches, paintings, furniture. There are extraordinarily large, colourful vessels, vases and pots from Burmantofts. Tables thick with books, divided into subject areas. Design. Opera, writing and sketching, photography.

It's all a tribute to Hockney's rampant imagination and breath-taking productivity. There's a huge distended chair in one corner, a typical Hockney challenge to linear design. A grey-haired woman is standing in front of it, her hand solicitously on the elbow of a blind woman with a black guide dog, her eyes closed, intently listening to her companion's reading of the information framed alongside the chair. I think of how wonderful that is, the relationship between these two women, the intensity of the listener, the way in which the Labrador's identity is one with the blind woman. He is there but not there at all, ready to guide. I wait for them to move away from the massive chair so I can take a picture but then I realise they *are* the picture and take it with them just on the verge of leaving the frame.

I buy a book of photographs. I want to buy Nicky a book of Hockney's work for her upcoming birthday, but she is feeling overwhelmed. She is slumped on a bench, tearful.

"I feel there's no colour in my life. What have I produced, compared to all this."

Upstairs on floor two, there's the kind of bookstore one could spend two hours in. I find a table full of books about epic walking in Yorkshire and Britain, from south to the north, books about rivers, insects, birds and trees. I buy the definitive study of Robins, the birds. A fatuous piece of egotism simply because I share the name, but I have always been interested in them. I believe that the souls of my closest friends and relations enter the Robins when they swarm me in Canada or Britain in spring. I talk to them. Rupert. How are you? Look at that handsome puffed out chest. David. My Father. Not the women. Odd?

We go upstairs to floor three, to The Arrival of Spring. It's a series of iPad paintings Hockney did every day of early 2011 of a single road near Bridlington in East Yorkshire. They are garish, harsh. The quality of the prints are almost day-glo. There's not the texture of paint, as if he is seeing nature through LSD glasses. Having spent all these months admiring the hundreds of variations of true nature on similar walks and roadways, and having just seen so many beautiful representations of this in his other work, I find "The Arrival of Spring" too techno-trippy. With most of these technological innovations, there's the early rush of seeing how much they can do. Wow. Look at this painting app on my iPad! How brilliant. I'm going to do a series of… this road, this road. Yes. It will be brilliant. Oh yes, David, brilliant.

No, David, not so brilliant. If the world is ever reduced to a great smoking, acridic trash dump and someone discovers your iPad strobing pics of nature, it will never bring it back.

One admires the volume and huge spectrum of his work. He is clearly a one-man industry and must be making absolute oodles of money, but what is his legacy, I am left wondering? Like Andrew Marvell in Hull, or van Gogh who died broke and uncelebrated, will his work stand up 100/200 years from now? I now doubt it.

In the car, on the way back, Nicky bemoans the lack of a jam-packed career to match her great talent. She would so much have liked to work more at a higher level. I console her with the observation that so many people never get to prove their talent the way she has. She has had that sensation (whatever it is I do not know) of performing at the Royal Academy and being told how stunning and "Wow" she is. I think this helps and we resolve to follow up on the idea of renting a theatre in London for a week for her one-woman show, 'Hooked'. After a while she puts her arm around my shoulders and lightly scratches my back.

"You're a good man," she says.

That's enough for me.

WEDNESDAY 19TH JULY

BIRDIE BINGE

Great golf day. Four birdies, won nine pounds.

The day the BBC salaries were revealed.

Played with Tony, against two Marks. The ex-hockey player and an Army veteran. Birdie the long sixth, putting in from the fringe.

The tenth, chip in from thirty yards up beyond the flag to a bank and trickles back down, plop. The fourteenth par three, seven iron to two feet. And the eighteenth, a 45 foot wiggler putt downhill to win the match.

Not much else makes me happier.

THURSDAY 20TH JULY

HENRI, AGAIN

Henri is visiting again. We talk and talk, walk and walk. We visit Rievaulx Castle, which I don't enjoy. Eight pounds fifty rather wasted. I get the architecture, the antiquity, but the details of a monk's life in 12th century Britain depress me. Potage was all they ate, they slept on mats, they would rise at two thirty or four am to pray. They worked like dogs. I think it's madness, a brutal and self-abusing life. It would have sent me galloping over the stone walls into the Garden of Eden surrounds, to the nearest tavern, wassail and wenches to boot. Religion, I am done with. Definitely, on balance in my lifetime, a creator of terrible bloodshed, suspicion and hatred. Definitely anti-progressive. The Maoists, and various Communists tried to crush religion, imprisoning believers. And of course that had the opposite effect, making the self-righteous buggers even more stubborn. Believers, ironically, don't have to prove anything. They have their Unknowable Gods, and repression just fuels their stubbornness.

And Martyrdom beats anonymity every time, even gives it a granite identity.

Nicky and Henri disappear into the Museum, for hours it seems.

Most of the time he is here they go off together while I watch The Open.

Many years ago Henri slept with a girl I was in love with, a rather French act of friendship. He later claims that in the act, she calls out my name! Ha! Years later I ask her about it and she says she was a victim to his seductive skills, which were not inconsiderable. Double Ha!

In the summer evening, we have a wonderful rabbit stew dinner on the deck. I get a bit hammered, deliciously so. Henri talks about a previous visit to Yorkshire at the age of seventeen, pursuing an exchange student he had met at German camp in the Schwarzwald.

"What was her name?

"I can't remember."

"Emma? Victoria?"

"No. I wish I could remember, but I can't."

"What did she look like?"

"Very, very nice."

"Red hair? Blue eyes? What can you remember?"

"Beautiful lady. She had freckles and big tits."

Nicky and Jules gag on their rabbit.

SATURDAY 22ND JULY

WHITE COAT FRENZY

Henri and Nicky head off to the Castle, I watch the Open.

Members of my Toronto golf pool litter shots all over Royal Birkdale. Charl Schwarzel, the buck-toothed chicken farmer's son from the Highveld, dies the death of a dozen near misses. From one shot off the lead, he tumbles. His usual laser-sharp drives scuttle inches into the short rough; his approach shots are a little bit off, and instead of being 18 inches out, his par putts are more than five feet out. Putts lip out, bogey follows bogey follows bogey, and he falls more than eight shots off the lead in what seems like ten minutes of TV airtime.

At twelve forty five, we go to cricket at Sheriff Hutton, a first X1 match. The other team has an umpire who seems very proud.

"Jack Shepherd," he says shaking my hand.

"Robin Hood," I reply.

"I'm not the sort of umpire who favours his own team," he declares.

He proudly announces that he was chosen Umpire of the Year, with a quote "92.5 percent average" unquote at the league dinner the previous year.

I reply, "I must tell you. I am completely unregistered. I've been living in Canada for forty years, but played a lot growing up in South Africa."

He taps the side of his head. "Once it's in here, it never goes away."

"I'd like to take a course. Are you licensed?"

He nods, but I'm not sure it's an answer to my question.

"I've been doing this for years. Last year I got a 92.5 percent rating. I could have umpired in the Senior League, but they take it too seriously. Here it's much more easy-going."

"May I ask you something?" I say. "How do you call a wide?"

"Oh it's up to you really."

Me, interrupting, instead of listening.

"I figure, if the batsman can't reach it, it's a wide."

He nods. "That's right."

"And a no ball. Is it above the waist, or above the head off slow bowlers?"

"Both," he says. Though just before first ball, he comes and says he's spoken to both captains and the rule shall be anything above the waist, today.

I leave the field briefly to let Nicky take a picture of Henri and I to send to Kenneth, my South African friend in Canada, and my sister Ann in South Africa. I say goodbye to Henri, we hug, and as I walk away to join the other umpire, he wishes me well in his French accent.

As we walk out to the middle, the umpire says, "Now you're bringing in foreigners." And apparently regretting the comment, immediately adds, "Not that I've got anything against foreigners, mind." Given me.

The first three overs are very tight. I see that Henri and Nicky are already assuming the positions of the comatic cricket-averse, and suddenly get up and go.

The Sheriff Hutton team cannot score any runs, with the exception of Molby the burly #3. The middle-aged seamer from my end is impressively accurate, varies his pace cleverly. Our opening batsman VJ swings across a straight ball and it hits him on the roll on the front foot. It's a savage appeal. I am not sure about whether it would have gone over the stumps or hit them. Not Out. But the decision gnaws at me. I turn down a second appeal where the ball is seaming down the leg.

Other than that I have nothing to do for three hours. Six balls are bowled, six stones go into my pocket. Stroll to square. Watch the big North Yorkshire pigeons drift and peak, and drop and wheel. A raptor hovers in the cornfield at the country end. My attention has to go to the ball. That few seconds of concentration, through to the keeper, I check back for the raptor but it has flown away. I keep getting twinges of ecstasy.

Late in the innings, the one batsman who is holding

out suddenly swirls, lets out a groan, and subsides to the ground at the Castle End. He's apparently overcome with the heat, or dehydration. He won't go off. Tough guy. When he gets down to my end, I offer him my water and he finishes it.

At tea, I refill my water bottle, grab a cup of the elixir of life and walk beside the pavilion for a smoke.

Gas cylinders and rollers lie in the uncut grass next to a rusty wire fence.

On the bench in front of the pavilion, one of the veteran players from the Wednesday team sits wearing an Aussie hat.

"It's not enough, is it?"

"What's that?"

"108."

He shakes his head. "Probably not."

I am not sure but I think this is a team not expecting to win, most of the time.

"What does one need in these (45 over) games?"

"140. 160."

He is friendly, with a wide face, and easy manner. And no Yorkshire accent. Just plain, globally understood, clear English.

I go over to the umpire, who has given out two of our batsmen with some relish. He has taken his white jacket off and is sitting in one of those silences that cover more of the game of cricket, at the village level, than does noise. Silent. Looking out at the pitch, and maybe the country and sky beyond. Does all this silence and space give comfort, and give comfort because part of us feel that this is what the other side sounds like?

"That went well, I thought."

'Nice game," he says. "You know, I am very neutral, very neutral. Known for it, I am." This seems to be the third time he has told me this. Begs the question.

"How long have you been umpiring?"

"Oooh, let me see. I retired when I was fifty and I'm seventy-five now. So that's twenty-five years."

There's a long pause.

I head into tea for a refill, a ham 'n' cheese sandwich and a strawberry tart.

The second innings is as incident-packed as the first was eventless. Our left arm opening bowler is following through, running well down the wicket. I mention it to him, and he stands on the pitch pointing out two white marks beyond the crease.

"As long as I am out after these marks, it's okay."

"Okay." I stand corrected.

The next ball, his follow-through, takes him down the pitch well beyond the marks.

I walk over at the beginning of the next over and his boots don't seem to me tearing up the clay-like track much at all, so I drop it. It's not a Test match.

A few balls later I hear an "ouch" behind me, and he has stopped. He has pulled his lip out and is gesturing, stung by something in his mouth. I go and inspect, thinking if it's a bee sting I can extract it, though I don't have tweezers at hand.

He pulls his lower lip as far down as possible and sure enough there's a white spot, but no sting pouch. I offer him the rest of my water. He swills and spits out.

"Are you allergic to bee stings?"

"I don't know. If I die, we'll find out."

There's a fast bowler for you.

The visitors are rattling along. Their opening batsman, a left-hander, misses a forward defensive prod from our high school leg spinner who is getting a lot of turn. The ball bounces outside off (no problem), turns in past the bat and hits him low on the front pad, which is halfway forward. There's a rather quiet appeal.

I look, and think, that's going to hit the wickets. And his pad is between the lines. I put my finger up.

The fielders shout with happy surprise, but the batsman throws his head back as if he's been shot in the face. The umpire at square leg seems agitated.

An over later, the new batsman is fooled by the inswing on the leggie and the ball hits him low on the ankle as he fiercely brings his bat down and strikes himself on the foot. There's another less than full-throated appeal. I am taken a little by surprise. I felt sure he would hit it. A skilled batsman would have clipped it off middle and leg through mid-wicket. But he didn't get his bat down in time. There's been a bit of a wait, but I believe the ball would have hit low middle and leg, no question. But did he hit it? No. He didn't. He's out. I raise my finger, again. There's a grunting sound from the other umpire. The batsman swerves away furiously, hitting his own pads with his bat in an explosive expression of anger and dissent.

The next over, our balding spin bowler draws their good mid-order batsman who is leading them to victory down the track and out of his ground. The young keeper sweeps the bails off and I give him out, stumped. At this point my finger feels hot.

Three decisions. All good. The next ball, the left handed batsman, who is open to me as I haven't moved across to square leg, flashes, there's a humungous click, the whole field goes up, but the old umpire doesn't move. There's a stunned moment before the batsman walks off, of his own accord. That's odd. I'm thinking. Was the other umpire actually not going to give him out?? The very next ball bowls the batsman. Hat trick. The visitors are now 75 for 6, and in trouble.

The next over the leggie bowls a beauty that lands on middle stump but cuts sharply away outside off stump. They all roar an appeal. "Not Out," I say emphatically.

This is where the trouble starts. The leggie now bowls a high ball outside leg stump and the batsman knocks it down to backward square leg for a four. The umpire at square leg is gesticulating with his arm. He wants me to signal no ball. I ignore him. The batsman reached it because he hit it. He turns to the mid wicket fielder and they confer. He is obviously saying it is a no ball and wants the whole field to know it.

As the fielders search for the ball, I walk towards to the

umpire and ten yards from him, in a very clear voice, I ask, "Do you, Mister Umpire, have a problem?"

I have reached him by now and am looming over him.

"It's your decision," he says, "but from here it seemed very high."

"Do you want me to change my decision?"

He shakes his head. This is not good. I am challenging a local master umpire, in his own mind, in my first important game. A little bird inside my head is screeching, but I cannot tell if it's in warning or in hysterics.

A few balls later and the leggie launches another full toss at the batsman who takes an almighty swish, and misses it, as the ball goes down leg for byes. I do not signal a wide because I feel the batsmen, having just hit a four off an identical ball, could have reached it. The umpire at square leg is now apoplectic, whirling his arms like a baby albatross knocked out of its nest. He then makes a gesture, arms spread as in, "WTF are you doing, you eegit?"

From then on to the end, I ignore this other umpire. But I stew. I have never seen one umpire show up another umpire publicly like that. Is that appropriate? Don't I own my end? Umpires don't clash. I decide he warrants a word.

His side wins fairly comfortably. 108 is nowhere near enough.

The umpire and I walk off with the stumps and bails, silent.

The players walk out shaking my hand, although two of theirs (the lbw victims?) will not look me in the eye or say anything. One lad clearly is radiating anti-respect. We get into the Umpire's Room and I say, "Is it appropriate in this league to show up the other umpire in public?"

He is clearly worried I am going to bring this up.

"Well, I know you saw things from your end the way you saw them but that second ball bounces way beyond the wicketkeeper."

"That may be so, in your opinion, but as I said earlier in my opinion the batsman could have reached it. Even so, even if I am wrong, is it appropriate to publicly express your criticism of another umpire?"

This clearly is too much for him, and he mumbles something inaudible, as he packs away his things.

I am finished and I leave saying, "No doubt our paths will cross again."

White Coat Frenzy.

I left thinking I may have blown it. He was always making notes. Is he going to report me to some higher authority in Yorkshire cricket? Is my joy at umpiring in Yorkshire about to be scandalously terminated? Methinks, his 92.5 percent is more important to him than some foreigner cummin' in here with his cockeyed umpiring. And French friends.

SUNDAY 23RD JULY

BARCELONA DANIEL AND BIRKDALE HUA TONG

Today my friend Daniel marries his Spanish sweetheart in Barcelona. Daniel is the top researcher at the Canadian Broadcasting Corporation from the time I became a radio reporter in the late seventies. For the next twenty years he provides me with amazing research on every topic I am assigned. Pollution in northern mines, the mafia, mesothelioma, El Salvador's guerrillas, evangelical bikers. He's encyclopaedic, fast, clinically objective. He is also one of the few golfers at the Corp and in the summers, we go out and play the cheap public courses around Toronto. He hits the ball miles with a whippy, rapid swing, but is never impressed by his own skills. Often disgusted by them, in fact. I remember him hitting a 90 foot putt perfectly, which curls in to the hole but stops on the lip. He shakes his head and curses. "Jesus, I was sure that would turn in more than that!"

Years later, after a lifetime of lip-outs on the matrimonial and romantic front, Daniel, a rail-thin cyclist is levelled by a drunken Porsche driver descending the Avenue Road hill in Toronto at midnight. He sustains multiple fractures and is laid up for months. Then he gets skin cancer. He recovers enough to attend a conference on public broadcasting, and falls for the Spanish translator. He invites me to the wedding in Barcelona but I decline because on that day, I have purchased a ticket for the most important and exciting day in the annual golfing calendar.

Clearly my values are all wrong, but it's incurable. I know he will forgive me.

The final round of the Open. The Open has always been the most exotic and coveted of golf's big events. Months ago I bought a fifty pound ticket to the last day of the 146th Open at Royal Birkdale, two and a half hours drive away from where I live.

I rise at Castle Howard at six am figuring I would get there for the end of Charl Schwarzel's round and Jon Rahm's tee-off at ten thirty five.

Nearing Southport, yellow AA signs point the way but one village amusingly features Halloween monsters, ghouls and ghosts. If I was a player this would unsettle me, like a local curse.

This is the threat of Open championship links golf. Demons lurk for most players today.

I park as directed and a ten-minute bus ships me to within a five minute walk. An entire village of royal blue has been constructed, the biggest building of which is

The Shop. One cannot enter the grounds without passing through The Shop. The corporate branding is ubiquitous, searing. It's almost as if they have to stamp your soul before you can enter the green fairways. It strikes me as a disappointing lapse in taste on the part of the Royal and Ancient, the organisers of the Open.

Inside the teeming Shop, it's Brands Unleashed. I didn't know there were so many brands in golf, and I hadn't expected this to be my first lesson of this hallowed Sunday. I go in and spot an XXL rain jacket, but it costs eighty five pounds. I have to get out right away. I emerge on the golf course side of the village, but battle to find an opening in the lines of people queuing up to Fedex their purchases back to the States. I feel I have escaped with only light burns.

The signposting is brilliant, like in a dream. I am here, the greatest day of the greatest tournament. The sun is shining, the wind is caressing my cheek, but I cannot find the game! It's like a recurring nightmare I have of getting an important tee-off time at a great course or tournament, but the car won't move, or something else, an endless herd of elephants at the crosswalk impedes me, or the road turns into toffee, things prevent me from getting there, and when I get there, everyone has gone home leaving a note flapping under a peg on the first tee.

"Couldn't wait. Sorry."

Back in Toronto, I have for years been a participant in a golf pool. Several of my picks have made it to the final round here and I am only really interested in following them, as opposed to the actual leaders.

I am just in time for Rahm, the star on my team this year. He's strolling down the first fairway munching on something. He could be a Spanish farmer in an apple orchard. My anti-corporate anxiety melts away. His ball is in light grassy rough about five yards from me, about 140 yards from the flag. He slowly and casually swings his club. There's the soft click of perfect contact. The ball is a blur. I feel cradled by his powerful tempo. But he's misjudged the wind. The ball lands on the green but trickles off into the fringey grass behind. He bogeys. His volcanic temper is not on display. Maybe he is on tranks, or the psychologist he has hired is helping. But he is out of it, fourteen shots behind the leader, the American wunderkind, Jordan Spieth. Frowning Spanish fans around me talk in hushed, concerned whispers. On the second hole he walks to his drive, munching something else, pulls his second shot and bogeys that one too. On the third tee he flips open a cooler and grabs a drink, swallowing it in two long draughts. Fifteen shots behind. I follow him for the first four holes but he seems disinterested and unmotivated. ("If I no ween, I no care"?) He seems to be eating the whole time. Does this mean he missed breakfast? Why is he missing breakfast? Is he up all night? These are the kinds of questions that dog the conscientious pool owner at a major. I drafted him on that cold January night on the 27th floor of that skyscraper in Toronto's business district to win this precise tournament, goddammit, and he's dogging it! Caramba. He pops something else in his mouth. Nuts? At this rate, the boy (he's only twenty) is going to have a weight issue.

I let him pass on with his following of worried Spanish rooks, then wait for the Belgian Bomber, Thomas Pieters, another poolie. I am also following players I have a bet on. I have betted Rahm, Pieters, Fleetwood and Leishmann, ten dollars each way, a chunk of the two hundred and thirty five pounds I won on Jeremy Corbyn.

I have never seen so many people at a sports event. They mill in a polite and quiet manner. The mounds and dunes between the holes make it almost perfect for this sort of spectacle.

And such a swathe of nationalities. Chinese, Aussies, Indians, Spaniards, Frenchmen, Italian, German, Kiwis, South Africans and of course lots of Britons. I hear quite a few strong Irish accents, too, here for Rory McIlroy, no doubt. The odd spectacularly dressed punter, brilliant multi-coloured checked suits that kind of thing, one bunch of men behatted with greens with pins on top. The British have this endearing habit of dressing like lunatics to big sport events.

Pieters swings the ball with great style and easy power, hits his drives long straight and true. But he putts clunkily, missing a series of makeable chances. His body begins to sag. He pouts like a handsome movie star who keeps getting passed over for the big roles.

On TV, the players seem calmly locked in. Live, I am

struck by how anxious and frustrated they are. Pieters' partner, Bubba Watson is a bag of twitches, arching and bending as if his body contains a jonesing cat. Troubled mumblings. He stands very erect to the ball, angled to the right and has slender, hairy forearms. He falls forward on most shots, and begs the ball almost immediately. "Oh pleeease." "Oh no, don't DO this to me." "Don't GOO there, pleeeease." "C-MAAAAN. F**k." He hits very few fairways and always blames something or someone else for his misfortunes. The wind, a mound, his caddy, a noise in the crowd. He comes across like a spoilt-brat who blames the outer world for robbing him of the perfection he feels is his birthright.

I am slightly disappointed in the design, the layout of the holes at Royal Birkdale. The first nine is all par fours and a couple of threes. I've got to have a par five in my nines. I can see the degree of difficulty, but they are much of a muchness. Long, surrounded by punitive rough and fescue, many, many bunkers. One dogleg after another. Slightly undulating greens. No spectacular holes. Rather repetitive. A test of endurance rather than an opportunity for brilliance. Best not to risk. Boring. Nowhere near as delicious as the courses I've played in the Irelands, for example. The Postage Stamp, the stepped par five at Lahinch with the ravine left of the pin. The ocean views. Not here. The course is hidden from the sea by huge dunes.

The food on offer is appalling. Five-alarm health alert. In time survivors will sue big events and the food industry for providing customers with food that can kill. Burgers, fish and chips, beer, waffles, ice cream. Not one healthy choice on hand. A vegetarian or salad bar would make a killing here, but the powers that be, the powers that be. Someone somewhere is keeping all the loot for him and his buddies. And they are no doubt McDonald's and KFC lobbyists and the like on the Board of Advisers or Regents. I eventually lump for a steak and ale pie, but as I reach the end of a long line up the woman behind the counter declares in a loud voice, "We are officially out of steak and ale pies."

Cornish pasty is available, but it's one of those English staples that I've always heard about but don't really know about. So I ask.

"Meat, onions, potatoes, gravy, luv."

"I'll 'ave wun of those then, darlin'."

I munch through most of me Cornish pasty, but it's basically heart attack food as well, heavy pastry dough with glutinous inner walls between the pastry and the lumpen, gelatinous meats therein. Or onions. Or whatever they are. There's a big screen showing that my poolies Stenson and Tony Finau are doing alright as is the goofy Aussie Marc Leishmann who is both a bet and a poolie. But, with Speith and Kuchar so far ahead I'm out of the money this year. The "Koo" sounds are being heard now as the leaders begin their well documented battle.

I have no interest in this duo. I have interest in very few American players. I actually have a conversation with a punter about this.

"Are you waiting for the big boys?" he asks.

"No. I don't really have any interest in the Americans."

"Me neither," he says, a local, a Scouser. "No sense of 'umour."

"I don't know what it is," I say.

"No sense of 'umour," he repeats.

It is true, I think, that the Americans seem to rely inordinately on Canadians for their laughs. Lorne Michaels. Jim Carrey. Mike Myers.

I decide to cease my rambling, and set myself down at an interesting location for a good spell. To continue on my theme of par fives making for more interesting golf, I head to the first of only two par fives at Royal Birkdale. The fifteenth, but the wind is against. I figure the wind will be behind the players on the par five seventeenth. More chance of seeing birdies and eagles.

After a bit of a wait, I get into the stand right behind the green. From here I can see the hole clearly, for 350 yards in front of the green below. All the players appear to drive over a big thick grass mound. Even if they find the rough to either side, they can hit their second shots onto the green. But they have to be very accurate. About seventy yards in front of the green, the fairway narrows considerably, and three rows of bunkers squeeze in in the available landing space. A pair of traps at 65 yards, thirty yards, and left and right of the flag.

Using my Made-In-China binoculars, I watch most of the field come in. Practically every player is putting for birdie or eagle. By now Thomas Pieters is in such a state that when he three putts for par, he hurls his club across the green, cartwheeling to a rest perfectly on his bag. He walks off and up to the 18th tee without watching to see what happens to Bubba. Bad for the kids, rude for your playing partner. I had thought he was ice-cool, that Belge.

Jason Dufner, an eccentric American, hits an absolutely exquisite 25 yard high bunker shot from my right, the second set of bunkers, over a high lip to check within three inches. As the green is triple-decked, he has to land it on the top deck and spin it back, which he does. He knows it's perfect, as do the whooping fans.

An English player called Southgate tops, or equators, his ball from the short rough about 250 yards right into my binoc lens, skimming over the bunkers right, and scuddering to a halt beneath me, a lucky shot, but one which enables him to birdie to minus-four, in sixth place. For him, a career finish (I read later he had thought he would never play again after testicular cancer, and that his father had played in an Open and done badly years ago). My fellow weighty South African, Ernie Els comes lumbering slowly down the fairway like a war-weary old bear, but with a sprightly twenty year old who is at six under for the round. The kid makes birdie and does a little dance. Huatong Li. From *China.* How does a twenty year old get all the way from China to be leading the Open in the clubhouse. This happens every year at The Open. An unknown gets into the mix. I look him up on my cell phone. He won three Asian tour events last year. At nineteen! One to watch for next year's pool. Leishmann shows up like an Aussie bus driver on hols, all aw shucks, hits it on the green from far back and puts an 80 foot putt just north of the hole, in for birdie and -5 for the round, -4 for the Open. Tied for fourth at that point. I'm in the money, just. If it holds.

One of his challengers, Paul Casey, is way back, the shortest driver so far, but on the fairway. Through my binocs I see him power an iron towards me, swivelling, and hitting it as hard as he can, for a short man.

The ball disappears into the sky, takes an eternity and then, plop, six feet under the flag. The shot of the day. The crowd cheers their countryman. But he curls the eagle putt left a smidgen. I know that putt is going to break that way as it is a common line in by earlier players. It's interesting that no one in the crowd calls out, "Breaks one and a half balls to the left, Paul," as he walks up to mark it. It would be critical info for the player, but not decorum.

I have to be part of the eighteenth fairway final act. I have watched it for more than forty years, back to Player and Nicklaus and Watson and Faldo, an Open signature, the walk to victory before the swarming spectators. It is the moment every year when the best golfer on the planet at that precise moment wins the best major. I am in amongst hundreds to the left of the fairway, about 100 yards out. A girl to my right is getting internet reception and reads off her phone, re Speith and Kuchar, "*both have driven into the rough at eighteen.*" Some drunken yahoos have clambered onto a row of big plastic garbage bins behind us, and a boozy man with a bent nose beneath them is trying to get one of the drunks off so he can have a perch. As Grace hits his bunker shot, they are yelling at each other and I initiate a loud ssssh that becomes punitive fast, and like guilty boys they hush.

The big yellow signboard registers Speith's birdie-eagle-birdie run and he moves two strokes up on Kuchar. People don't cheer. Then Kuchar's number is taken down. The -9 is pulled in, and people go oooooh. Then a one is put in and people start to cheer and raise their voice when the zero is added. Kooooo starts up. One stroke behind Speith. It sounds like people are just doing it because they like the sound it makes. I don't think they are particularly enamoured of Kuchar. But moments later Spieth's second one on the minus-11 is taken out and changed to a two. Minus-12. Two stroke lead, one to play. A Victory march. In fact once again as the two Americans pass by, all you hear is "KOOOO". I think it's silly, rude like a lame meme. Speith must have done a salvage job somewhere back there after his wobbly beginning. He's seized the moment. Good for him. Golfing immortality is made of such comebacks.

Leishmann's -4 keeps him at sixth. I've won twenty two on him, lost sixty overall.

There are so many people to get out of there. Eventually I get back to my car. It takes an hour and a half of stop and go traffic to clear Southport. Once I do, I have to drive through rain on the highway but am sustained by a brilliant program on BBC Two, three hours of Claire Somebody playing music from the forties and fifties.

Nat, Ella, Judy Garland, Count Basie and Sinatra at the Sands.

"Come Fly With Me."

I make it home exactly at the time my GPS predicted, 11:08pm.

I loved the final day of The Open. But that box is checked and I'll never do it again. Or maybe next year. Carnoustie, a beast of a course.

FRIDAY 28TH JULY
HAUNTED HALL

In North Yorkshire, one stumbles into the most amazing things.

I take Nicky to a riding stables to arrange her birthday present. Lacy's Cottage Riding School is just outside the village of Scrayingham. We meet Chris Pimlott, a total horse man and he books her in.

On the way there, we pass a bridge with footpath signs, and return there with Sophie the beagle for a walk. It turns out to be the entrance to Howsham Hall. We walk up there and the sheep fields give way to manicured grass and a square grey stone stately home. We see no sign of habitation. It has many small square leaded windows and seems to stare bleakly back at us.

This is how knowledge travels. Nicky googles Howsham Hall. It's been for sale for five million pounds, but no takers. It carries a curse. Apparently the beams to build it in 1610 were lifted from nearby Kirkham Priory destroyed when Henry VIII dissolved all the monasteries. According to the curse, "all male heirs of the estate will perish and true happiness will never come to that family or its successors." This turns out to be the case, with successive owning families failing to produce male heirs over the centuries.

In the 1950s, it is bought by a man called Knock and turned into an exclusive private boys boarding school. Knock apparently is notoriously strict, known for entering mistakes in a little black book. He would run up and down the sidelines at sports events, yelling, "It's in the book. It's in the book," at pupils who err. Three former pupils claim they were abused at the school, but other pupils speak in defence of Mr Knock and his institution.

However, due to dwindling attendance the school is closed in 2007.

It's now for sale.

The place looks unpeopled and its seven multi-paned bay windows stare forlornly, as we make our way down the lane and back to 2017.

SATURDAY 5TH AUGUST

THE WILTING PROTEAS

One of the great experiences of the past twenty six years, since South Africa is readmitted to international cricket, is watching the national team fight to the top of world cricket with powerful batting, devastating fast bowling and electrifying fielding. The current team arrives here for the summer tour with high expectations as the number one test team in the world. But so far, this summer, they've been dreadful.

I am heading to Old Trafford for my final big sport event of the summer, a ticket I bought in the promise of spring, the second day of the fourth test. In the series, the Proteas have already crumpled to a 1-2 deficit. Their batting, especially, is woeful, apart from an 80 by the sublime but erratic Hashim Amla and a dogged, bruised 130 by the Welkom grinder, Dean Elgar. The bowling, apart from a few glorious overs from Philander and Morkel lacks venom. The fielding is, at times, atrocious.

I walk miles from my parking lot, under the darkly named

Moscow Tunnel of the Manchester United ground, past illuminated ovals of the great and tragic history of the Red Devils. The architecture, like Headingley, is disappointing. Grey concrete and red steel angles, no grace or fluidity.

The cricket ground has three big Walmart-sized Red Boxes plonked down at three corners, and apart from the customary green hallowed turf is a functional, modern, soulless structure.

The South Africans make heavy work of the last three England wickets, and Johnny Bairstow manufactures a wonderful, strike-farming 99. I am sitting crammed in my seat down at backward square leg as he faces Maharaj with one run to go for his century. The huge screen shows pictures of his mum and sister nervously looking on. (Bairstow is heir to a heart-rending tragedy. His father, a much-loved teammate of Geoff Boycott's at Yorkshire, about the only Yorkshire teammate Boycott seems not to have disliked, committed suicide when his son was eight.)

I see SA has one man at deep backward square, and another at midwicket. I have one of those premonitions. There's Big Space there. He's going to sweep to bring up his hundred. That's what I would do. And, he does exactly that the very next ball, but misses it. That tiny little scintilla of whoops might have gone through his brain as he dropped down to play the shot. In an event like this, one minute there's such a tumult of noise and singing from the crowd, the next, pin-dropping quiet. The ball strikes him on his front pad which is well down the wicket, but the umpire, gutsily, and to the outrage of the masses, raises his finger. Inevitably, Bairstow reviews, but it is upheld. The umpire is right, by a whisker.

South Africa starts their innings while I am outside circling the stadium and inspecting the crowds, and Anderson, probably one of the great two-way swing bowlers of all time, traps Elgar plumb lbw third ball. I hear it on my BBC radio earpiece, and the stands above me erupt with a joyous roar.

In his brief, caressing tenure Amla looks wonderful but is "strangled" down the legside, caught behind off Roland-Jones. Bavuma digs in at #4, but Heino Kuhn looks awful. Disgraceful innings. Chopping, hacking, chinese-cutting. Du Plessis replaces him and in three balls Anderson has both his and Bavuma's bails a-spinning. De Kock looks like a fish out of water. If he can't attack, he's lost. Caught driving at slip off Ali, the offspinner.

I sit in a new seat, way up behind the bowler's arm at the Brian Statham Stand end, and vocally berate the defeatist South Africans as they drag their bats in and out. To Kuhn as he mopes back to the pavilion.

"Go home, Kuhn." How quickly I descend to boorish condemnation. In Roman coliseums I would have been one of those louts sliding my finger across my throat. Off with his head.

For me, it's the second low point in a lifelong love of the team.

The first, when I am a boy, is Jackie McGlew's team. Listening on shortwave radio to terrible, scratchy players with the inferiority complex that afflicts white South

Africans on the world stage. The high point of that era is when McGlew, a diminutive, defensive opening batsman bats forever. Nine and a half hours for a century. When this is your greatest achievement you are definitely second division. At school I hit him for six. Serves him right.

Then the glory years of my generation, the Pollocks, Richards and Procter, the deserving boycott wilderness, and then Gibbs, Smith, Kallis, Donald, Ntini, early and mid-Amla.

This current version of the team has comprehensively collapsed. The future of the game now lies with its two black stars, Rabada and Bavuma, who will be the next captain, one senses.

I leave early, back through the abandoned canyons of Manchester's glory arenas.

SUNDAY 6TH AUGUST

ACCUSED!

If the South African cricket season is winding down to a crushing 3-1 defeat, it seems my golfing happiness is also about to get a kick in the nuts.

It starts on Wednesday when Barry Moment, the congenial guy who organises the Clutch warns me that the Club Championship, which I am entered into the upcoming Sunday, is two rounds in one day. I am vaguely aware of this fact, but had thought nothing of it, other than I would be at the golf course the entire day of my daughter's second day here. I detect a certain agitation as he conveys this 'warning' to me, but as I walk up to five hours in a day I am in no way awed by the physical challenge. But his tone is odd.

After my round, as I enter the clubhouse to submit my score (63 net with Dave, an MP built like a brick shithouse, a very competitive ten handicapper), the club Secretary, which I have learned is an all-powerful position in the hierarchy of the Yorkshire golf club, emerges to tell me I have to get a move on.

"Have I been accused of slow play?" I ask.

"Yes."

There's a pause while I let this slight seep in.

"Never happened before."

"Well, you can't play four hour rounds."

I have no idea how long my round has taken.

He goes on. "Do you know the club championships is two rounds? We can't have four hour rounds."

"Okay."

Today I show up for the club championship for my twenty past eight tee off. I am paired with two twentysomethings, one, a lanky, Ian Poulter-like lad who works at the local hybrid bus factory and has a four month old baby boy. And Sam, a stocky ex-footballer. After a pleasant round, we finish at about eight minutes past twelve. Three hours and forty eight minutes. I shower and have a coronation chicken, and change. Getting ready for our next tee-off time at eight minutes past one, I see the club Secretary coming down the walkway towards me and greet him warmly.

Not reciprocated.

"Robin," he says, then growls, "You've got to move it along."

"What? Wait a minute."

He stops. Three other groups waiting to tee-off listen in.

"Are you accusing me of slow play? Again?"

"Yes."

"It's just not true. I have never been accused of slow play in all my years playing golf. Who is making these allegations?"

"We can't have four hour rounds."

"I'm sorry I just don't accept this. I'm the guy in Canada pushing everyone else to speed up. No way am I slow!"

I'm pissed, showing it, the other golfers are looking on, but so is he, red-faced, facing me down. Fools confronting each other about a technicality. This is how wars start.

"Look here," he says. "You are trailing sixty yards behind your playing partners."

I was?

Holy shit. Am I being watched? And blamed?

Feebly, I bleat.

"I'm sixty six, man."

He murmurs something unsympathetic.

This throws me. In the second round I rush, telling the other guys I am just going to hit when ready. I mishit poorly planned shots, littering strokes over par. The lanky one says he never saw my play as slow, as does Sam. He asks the group behind. No problem with them either. Nobody has ever mentioned this to me, except said Secretary but I am tarred, and publicly so. I have a really nauseating feeling. What can it be?

I finish the tournament. We finish at four forty three. That's three and a half hours. I play okay, 74/80 net.

Last night I fret about this and cannot sleep.

Then I think back and realise none of the older guys from the Clutch seem to be playing in the club championship. Maybe that's the issue? It's ageist. He doesn't want older, 16 handicappers playing in the club championship at all. I think back on all the Clutch matches and the match I played in Leeds for the club and no one ever mentions slow play.

On waking this morning I google 'how long does it take to play a round of golf'. The consensus is, from half a dozen websites… FOUR hours.

What do I do?

Perspective, Benger.

You've been threatened by cabinet ministers, doctors of law and medicine, witchdoctors, revolutionaries, criminals, generals, and murderers.

There's no way a golfing bullyboy is going to unsettle you.

But he has got his point across brutally clearly. For the rest of the season I am faster.

With the exception of the grumpy club Secretary, I look back over the golf, the cricket, the whole summer in Yorkshire with gratitude. I am grateful for the opportunity to spend more than two weeks visiting a place. Living in it. Exploring it. Finding the place beautiful, inspirationally so, and the people really friendly, original, proud, helpful and interesting.

I ask my friend Jules why it's so, well, nice. Why the people are so great? She says their sense of independence is important. And their belief that they do actually live in "God's Own Country."

But there is a hardness here. They can be tough. I felt it that first week off Geoff Boycott. They won't be told what to feel or think, even when they might be wrong. And if you are an outsider, tough. Tomorrow I'll be gone. They will die here, and, in most cases, they look back on generations of their own family.

Like everywhere I've spent a lot of time, South Africa as an English boy, Canada as a South African exile, you can't just become one of them because you want to.

THURSDAY 10TH AUGUST

COMMUNISM AND THE POLISH WAITRESS

It's the end of the summer. The PGA championship has started. I bet on Rahm, Pieters, Hoffman C, Johnson Z and the 200-1 outsider Hua Ton Li, the Chinese twenty year old who did so well at The Open. If he wins I get three thousand, one hundred pounds.

There's no Wednesday cricket match. The weather clears from a downpour on Tuesday but last week was the last fixture of that league. I am a little sad. I like doing it for eighteen overs each side. Two hours in the evening, beneath the ruined castle at Sheriff Hutton. But I am on for the Saturday game at York.

Last night we watched Jane Eyre, one of the most beautifully shot films I have seen. The director of photography is Adriano Goldman, a Brazilian music video maker! More than half a dozen times I had an intake of breathe at his opening shots in many of the scenes. Like paintings.

We have now been joined by son Griffin, from London, and daughter Tess from Toronto. We walk, then nap then make dinner and someone picks a film. It's lovely to have them, though I look forward to being alone again, here and there, in a few weeks. They all have actively critical intelligences.

My son and I drive to Terrington to pick up a cappuccino and the newspaper.

My son, who departed formal education in his early teens for a life in cyberspace, becomes interested in the real world through movies. He has recently watched The Deer Hunter and has asked me about Vietnam.

"Oh, it was about Communism."

We take a table outside, in the sun.

"So what is Communism?" he asks.

I feel fatigue come over me. But I attempt a less than authoritative explanation.

"It must start with a story about my university days," I say.

He looks at me patiently. From past experience I know I must capture his attention, before the eyes glaze over.

"At the age of eighteen, in South Africa, I was the privileged of the privileged. A white male."

(Jesus, is he thinking, another how-I-brought-down apartheid-Dadstory?)

"I was the top boy in the most expensive school in the country, but by the time I was in my second year at university I knew it all had to come tumbling down.

The hostility and unhappiness was suffocating. In the very body language of the black people. Because Communism was such an incendiary idea for their empowerment, the apartheid government tried to wipe it out. There was a law called the Suppression of Communism Act. Another part of this nationwide ban was that books about Communism were banned except for restricted academic study. I was studying politics and got permission to take out the Communist Manifesto, a tatty green hardback book. It was a book written by a German called Karl Marx in the mid 1800s. Communism is defined in this slim volume. To get it out, I had to sign a government form, giving my name and address, explaining what I needed it for. A librarian unlocked a glass case, and handed me the book for forty eight hours. I read it in one sitting and thought, yes, this is the solution. The principles of Christianity, which I had believed in up to that point, are also beautifully simple and fair to all. But in reality, the Anglican Church was wishy-washy at that time. It was mostly the church of rich white English South Africans. Our black servants had evangelical meetings in their own poor areas. Religion was not the solution in South Africa. After all, the government was stuffed with religious people who justified systemic racism throughout the land."

As we talk, a flock of pupils in dark green uniforms, from the private school across the road, walk into the teashop.

The mothers, in their dark glasses, coming to pick them

up were Yorkshire money. Range Rovers, Mercedes and Volvos abound.

"At the time of Karl Marx," I continue, "agriculture had been characterised by serfdom, slaves, unpaid work on farms owned by rich families. Then the Industrial Revolution came along with wages and working conditions for millions that were unbearable. So Marx formulated this idea that the workers should take over the farms and factories, the means of production; that is, that the workers should form committees that ran the process and owned the products they made. This worker control was, and still is, anathema to the owners and so-called capitalists, the rich individuals or families who drew the line at giving up ownership and control of lands and factories to committees of workers."

Griffin lights a cigarette and sips his coffee. He is paying me the kind of attention that he rarely has before. I have been, quite understandably, a luddite in his virtual world.

He has not shown much interest in subjects dear to my heart, like politics or ideology. In the end I had welcomed the fact his eyes would glaze over whenever I ranted or riffed about politics. A curbing influence.

I seize on this opportunity.

"Communism also means controlling government, as well as the economy. That governments should be set up by the people and for the people. That education and health should be a basic right for everyone. Parts of the communist manifesto are extremely persuasive: equality is the basic idea. Equality of opportunity, equality of men and women, of all races. But it wasn't keen on religion. Religion, Marx said, is the opium of the people, keeping them enslaved and compliant to the owner-capitalist class. It also doesn't shy away from militancy, the use of weapons to overthrow ruling elites. So throughout the world, wherever there was suffering or inequality of people on a massive basis, where a few held all the money and power, communism spread like wildfire. China, Russia, and eventually Africa and South America. Around the world, the ruling and owning classes saw Communism as the end of life as they knew and enjoyed it. Both sides accumulated weapons to protect or enforce their interests. Much blood has been shed over this."

"So what do you believe in?" he says. With son to father directness.

"Well, that was almost fifty years ago. My incredible experience of this world has taught me many other things. Mostly that human weakness, maybe human nature, frustrates any monopolising ideology. Communism became an ideology which caused tremendous suffering and devastating restrictions of freedom. In Russia, under Stalin, millions were starved to death in the name of Communist nation-building. It means that the state provides the basic needs of the people. In China, millions died in the name of Mao's socialism. And when you jail religious people, it does not wipe out Communism's biggest obstacle. Religion. Instead it makes rock-hard martyrs. Also, Communist strongmen took charge and created cults of leadership. To stay in power they became paranoid and vicious, bugging people, jailing and beating them. The voices of the masses were muzzled. Human rights became more of an appealing philosophy to me, a test of both capitalist and communist societies. And then my view of the rich softened. One learns about philanthropy. That there are certain individuals who have the gift for creating massive amounts of wealth, and although most rich people choose to hoard their millions, there are some entrepreneurs who do tremendous good. I mean Bill Gates has apparently given millions of dollars to reverse the AIDS epidemic. Or guys like Elon Musk, who push the electric car. I believe the best of them want to do good things. So for me, I like the idea of a society, like Canada, that encourages and backs visionary business people. But I have also decided that government should exist to serve the people and protect the poor. However there's a problem with how that affects people, which you see in this country. I mean, Jeremy Corbyn. You know who he is?"

"Of course."

"He's a socialist. Socialism is a milder form of communism."

"Okay."

"And he feels government should serve the majority. Free education and health. Help the poor. But you see even here, in North Yorkshire, in places like Leeds and Scarborough, in some downtown neighbourhoods, men of our ages doing nothing. It's called the nanny state or the welfare state. When you have welfare, unemployment insurance, there are people who would rather not work at all. Who will spend their lives living off the state. There seem to be a lot of people here, overweight, eating bad food, waddling around from the pub to the betting shop to the supermarket and back to the couch and TV."

He squints into the sun, taking this all in.

A trio of cyclists have taken the table near us. Even though their energy is admirable, I think they look ridiculous in their garish tights, like LSD pyjamas.

"Carry on," he says.

The thought comes to me that my thirty two year old son has never had a job. He is a millionaire poker player. It used to drive me crazy. He is so intelligent. But he's done so well, so much better than I did so Shut-Up Dad. He's very loving, and has been his own man since the age of fourteen, when he toured Norway, China and Brazil as a wealthy videogame phenom, signing autographs in far-flung shopping malls.

"Also, and this applies to my wanderings here…" I look around at the perfect, green, quiet village, the trees and the flowers. "Nature is the only thing I worship now, though worship is not quite the right word. I mean, how do you explain this sky, the sun, these woods and valleys, the earth, people, creation, this beautiful balance? I don't know. But nature rolls on, creating life relentlessly. New, beautiful, and sometimes tragic."

He nods thoughtfully.

There's a long pause.

"Is that okay?"

"Yeah," he says thoughtfully, nodding his head, "that's great."

The cyclists clip on and spin off down the road.

"Let's go home, to the girls."

"Yeah."

As we walk back to the car, I think about it.

"So to answer your question. I'm a hybrid, I guess. A socialist, naturist, entrepreneurist, humanist. And a cricketist."

"Cricketeer," he says.

Because of my daughter's interest in her mother's love of the Brontes and the moor scenes in the film last night, we head to Rosedale Abbey for a moors walk. They gasp as it comes into view, covered in purple.

We walk along the old rail track past the ruins of the seven hundred year old iron mine, out past the occasional horse rider, cyclist and walkers, though an infestation of mites, and back, looking down on that fabulous valley.

The women head back early and text us from the White Horse Farm Inn, halfway down the hill.

We are sitting outside, on the veranda and the waitress approaches. She is a slender, blonde-haired girl.

"Where are you guys from?" she says. Accent.

"Canada."

"Ooh that's such a long away from here," laughing.

"And you?"

"I'm from Poland."

"How did you get this job?" Nicky asks.

"Ooooh… On the internet I applied to everywhere. This place was live-in. It's so beautiful, no? You have chosen a good day. It rains all the time. And I cannot leave. There is one bus. Monday eleven o'clock. Oooh I went to Leeds. It took me so long. I didn't want to leave."

"Where in Poland?" I ask.

"A city. You won't hear of it. Wroclaw. It's also called Breslau. Very German city. Mostly Germans. Two hours from Berlin."

"So you speak German and Polish?" my wife asks.

"No no no German. Just Polish."

"And English."

"No, my English is better, but I am learning," she laughs, eruptions of good cheer. "Oh my god. My first day here I was so sad. I couldn't understand my boss. I couldn't understand my first order. The people here they speak English with…" And she rounds her mouth, making unintelligible noises. "But I like it here. But if you are here, you must go to Poland. It is so cheap. That beer will cost one pound in Poland. But here I am making lots of money. In Poland they pay two pounds."

"An hour?"

"A day!" She laughs again and again. Her laughter bubbles, uplifts. "But it is so beautiful here, no? Look at that."

She gestures to the valley and the sheep and the ridge before us.

"What would you like?" she asks.

She takes our order with great good humour and hustles across the gravelly ground back into the inn.

"She's lovely," says my wife.

"Champagne spirit," I say. "Just the kind of hard working person Brexiters want to bar."

So it ends. A family of four, munching happily on scampi and fish and chips in the glorious sunshine. Yorkshire looks as perfect as a postcard. They are sharing my new love.